Psalms

Tehillim תְּהִלִּים

Proverbs

מִשְׁלֵי Mishlei

Psalms
Tehillim תְּהִלִּים
Proverbs
Mishlei מִשְׁלֵי

David H. Stern

Lederer Books
A division of
Messianic Jewish Publishers
Clarksville, MD

2020   5

ISBN-13: 978-1-936716-69-2

Library of Congress Control Number: 2013940894

Lederer Books
A division of
Messianic Jewish Publishers
6120 Day Long Lane
Clarksville, Maryland 21029

Distributed by Messianic Jewish Publishers and Resources
Order line: (800) 410-7367
lederer@messianicjewish.net
www.messianicjewish.net

Printed in the United States of America

"Come! Let us sing to the LORD, let us blow the shofar to the Rock of our Salvation. Let us greet him with thanksgiving, with praiseful songs let us pray to him. For a great God is the LORD, and a great King above all heavenly powers."

(This prayer, read before reading and reciting the Psalms, prepares us to experience all the words of the Psalmist.)

Psalms *Tehillim* תְּהִלִּים

Some say that Psalms, the most often read section of the Tanakh ("Old"er Testament), is the Songbook of Israel. In a way, this is correct, but there's more.

For 3,000 years these words have been read, sung, and meditated on in order to give solace, provide expression of joy and fear, and help the reader hear what's in his or her own heart.

Attributed mostly to King David, a musician, many psalms include what might be called, in today's world of music, orchestration. Specific instruments are mentioned, mostly stringed instruments, to accompany the singing or recitation of these spiritual poems. As with music today, these ancient instruments added to the emotional impact the words had on their hearers. Additionally, some psalms begin with instructions to those who lead the time of singing and worship. These are found at the beginning of a psalm.

Especially in Hebrew, the Psalms provide clear imagery of what the writer was seeing and experiencing. Powerful statements are made, often not using verbs. Parallel sentences, in which the second part of the couplet echoes the meaning of the first, reinforce the psalmist's thoughts. Use of repetition for rhythm and emphasis drives home the intent of the author.

The Psalms express the majesty of God, along with a sense of God's nature as a shepherd. God is thus the transcendent creator, as well as the personal caretaker. No collection of writings has captured so well these two aspects of our Father.

For millennia, Jews and Christians, especially, have found references to the Messiah in the Psalms, experienced the depression of David as well as his sense of victory in God, and have found voice for the longing of their own souls.

Many commentaries have been written on the Psalms collectively, as well as each psalm individually. Having some historical background to them is helpful toward fully grasping their meaning. Yet, they can be read without this since they speak so universally of the human condition and the relationship between God and humanity.

Some psalms can be identified, such as the psalms of thanksgiving (e.g., Ps 30), hymns of praise (e.g., Ps 117) and royal psalms, probably used in coronations and weddings. Some psalms are prayers, such as Psalm 72, "The prayers of David son of Jesse are ended." The dominant theme of the Psalms is lament (expressions of complaint and pleas for help from God).

In Jewish usage, the Book of Psalms is divided, like the Torah, into five books, each closing with a praise or blessing.

The first book comprises the first 41 psalms. While Davidic authorship cannot be confirmed for all of them, this probably is the oldest section of the Psalms.

The second book consists of the next 31 Psalms (42–72), eighteen ascribed to David.

The third book contains seventeen Psalms (73–89), of which Psalm 86 is ascribed to David, Psalm 88 to Heman the Ezrahite, and Psalm 89 to Ethan the Ezrahite.

The fourth book also contains seventeen Psalms (90–106), of which Psalm 90 is ascribed to Moses, and Psalms 101 and 103 to David.

The fifth book contains the remaining 44 Psalms. Of these, 15 are ascribed to David, one (Psalm 127) as a charge to Solomon. Psalm 136 is generally called "the great Hallel," but the Talmud also includes Psalms 120–135. Psalms 113–118 constitute the Hallel, which is recited on the three great feasts (Passover, Weeks, and Tabernacles); at the new moon; and on the eight days of Hanukkah. Psalms 120–134 are referred to as Songs of Ascents, and were sung as the Jewish people went up to Jerusalem, as well as climbed up to the Temple.

According to Jewish tradition, the Psalms were actually sung in front of the Tabernacle, and then later during the reign of King Solomon when the Temple was completed, from its steps. The singers came from the tribe of Levi (Levites), and it was exclusively their privilege—non-Levites were not allowed to sing in that area of the Temple.

Psalms are used throughout traditional Jewish worship. Many complete psalms and verses from various psalms appear in the morning services. Psalm 145 (commonly referred to as "Ashrei" (Happy), is read three times every day and often begins worship services.

You are invited to join the authors of the Psalms, to experience many facets of human life—joy, depression, fear, anger, happiness, and love for God. Feel their range of emotions and let their words deepen your faith and enjoyment of life.

Tehillim
PSALMS

Book I: Psalms 1–41

1 ¹ How blessed are those
who reject the advice of the wicked,
don't stand on the way of sinners
or sit where scoffers sit!
² Their delight
is in *Adonai*'s *Torah*;
on his *Torah* they meditate
day and night.
³ They are like trees planted by streams —
they bear their fruit in season,
their leaves never wither,
everything they do succeeds.

⁴ Not so the wicked,
who are like chaff driven by the wind.
⁵ For this reason the wicked
won't stand up to the judgment,
nor will sinners
at the gathering of the righteous.
⁶ For *Adonai* watches over
the way of the righteous,
but the way of the wicked
is doomed.

2 ¹ Why are the nations in an uproar,
the peoples grumbling in vain?
² The earth's kings are taking positions,
leaders conspiring together,
against *Adonai*
and his anointed.
³ They cry, "Let's break their fetters!
Let's throw off their chains!"

4   He who sits in heaven laughs;
    Adonai looks at them in derision.
5   Then in his anger he rebukes them,
    terrifies them in his fury.
6   "I myself have installed my king
    on Tziyon, my holy mountain."

7   "I will proclaim the decree:
    ADONAI said to me,
    'You are my son;
    today I became your father.
8   Ask of me, and I will make
    the nations your inheritance;
    the whole wide world
    will be your possession.
9   You will break them with an iron rod,
    shatter them like a clay pot.'"

10 Therefore, kings, be wise;
    be warned, you judges of the earth.
11 Serve ADONAI with fear;
    rejoice, but with trembling.
12 Kiss the son*, lest he be angry,
    and you perish along the way,
    when suddenly his anger blazes.
    How blessed are all who take refuge in him.

3 ¹⁽⁰⁾ A psalm of David, when he fled from Avshalom his son:

2(1) ADONAI, how many enemies I have!
      How countless are those attacking me;
3(2) how countless those who say of me,
      "There is no salvation for him in God."   (*Selah*)

4(3) But you, ADONAI, are a shield for me;
      you are my glory, you lift my head high.
5(4) With my voice I call out to ADONAI,
      and he answers me from his holy hill.   (*Selah*)

6(5) I lie down and sleep, then wake up again,
      because ADONAI sustains me.
7(6) I am not afraid of the tens of thousands
      set against me on every side.

---

* or: Kiss purely

8(7)   Rise up, ADONAI!
         Save me, my God!
         For you slap all my enemies in the face,
         you smash the teeth of the wicked.
9(8)   Victory comes from ADONAI;
         may your blessing rest on your people.   (Selah)

4 1(0) For the leader. With stringed instruments. A psalm of David:

2(1)   O God, my vindicator!
         Answer me when I call!
         When I was distressed, you set me free;
         now have mercy on me, and hear my prayer.

3(2)   Men of rank, how long will you shame my honor,
         love what is vain, chase after lies?   (Selah)
4(3)   Understand that ADONAI sets apart
         the godly person for himself;
         ADONAI will hear when I call to him.
5(4)   You can be angry, but do not sin!
         Think about this as you lie in bed,
         and calm down.   (Selah)
6(5)   Offer sacrifices rightly,
         and put your trust in ADONAI.

7(6)   Many ask, "Who can show us some good?"
         ADONAI, lift the light of your face over us!
8(7)   You have filled my heart with more joy
         than all their grain and new wine.
9(8)   I will lie down and sleep in peace;
         for, ADONAI, you alone make me live securely.

5 1(0) For the leader. On wind instruments. A psalm of David:

2(1)   Give ear to my words, ADONAI,
         consider my inmost thoughts.
3(2)   Listen to my cry for help,
         my king and my God, for I pray to you.
4(3)   ADONAI, in the morning you will hear my voice;
         in the morning I lay my needs before you
         and wait expectantly.

5(4)   For you are not a God
         who takes pleasure in wickedness;
         evil cannot remain with you.

6(5)   Those who brag cannot stand before your eyes,
        you hate all who do evil,
7(6)   you destroy those who tell lies,
        ADONAI detests men of blood and deceivers.

8(7)   But I can enter your house
        because of your great grace and love;
        I will bow down toward your holy temple
        in reverence for you.
9(8)   Lead me, ADONAI, in your righteousness
        because of those lying in wait for me;
        make your way straight before me.
10(9)   For in their mouths there is nothing sincere,
        within them are calamities,
        their throats are open tombs,
        they flatter with their tongues.
11(10) God, declare them guilty!
        Let them fall through their own intrigues,
        For their many crimes, throw them down;
        since they have rebelled against you.

12(11) But let all who take refuge in you rejoice,
        let them forever shout for joy!
        Shelter them; and they will be glad,
        those who love your name.
13(12) For you, ADONAI, bless the righteous;
        you surround them with favor like a shield.

6 $^{1(0)}$ For the leader. With stringed instruments. On *sh'minit* [low-pitched musical instruments?]. A psalm of David:

2(1)   ADONAI, don't rebuke me in your anger,
        don't discipline me in the heat of your fury.
3(2)   Be gracious to me, ADONAI,
        because I am withering away;
        heal me, ADONAI,
        because my bones are shaking;
4(3)   I am completely terrified;
        and you, ADONAI — how long?
5(4)   Come back, ADONAI, and rescue me!
        Save me for the sake of your grace;
6(5)   for in death, no one remembers you;
        in Sh'ol, who will praise you?

7(6)   I am worn out with groaning;
        all night I drench my bed with tears,

8(7) flooding my couch till it swims.
My vision is darkened with anger;
it grows weak because of all my foes.

9(8) Get away from me, all you workers of evil!
For *Adonai* has heard the sound of my weeping,
10(9) *Adonai* has heard my pleading,
Adonai will accept my prayer.
11(10) All my enemies will be confounded,
completely terrified;
they will turn back
and be suddenly put to shame.

7 $^{1(0)}$ A *shiggayon* of David, which he sang to *Adonai* because of Kush the Ben-Y'mini:

2(1) *Adonai* my God, in you I take refuge.
Save me from all my pursuers, and rescue me;
3(2) otherwise, they will maul me like a lion
and tear me apart, with no rescuer present.

4(3) *Adonai* my God, if I have caused this,
if there is guilt on my hands,
5(4) if I paid back evil to him who was at peace with me,
when I even spared those who opposed me without cause;
6(5) then let the enemy pursue me
until he overtakes me
and tramples my life down into the earth;
yes, let him lay my honor in the dust. (*Selah*)

7(6) Rise up, *Adonai*, in your anger!
Arouse yourself against the fury of my foes.
Wake up for me; you commanded justice.
8(7) May the assembly of the peoples surround you;
may you return to rule over them from on high.
9(8) *Adonai*, who dispenses judgment to the peoples,
judge me, *Adonai*, according to my righteousness
and as my integrity deserves.
10(9) Let the evil of the wicked come to an end,
and establish the righteous;
since you, righteous God,
test hearts and minds.
11(10) My shield is God,
who saves the upright in heart.

12(11) God is a righteous judge,
a God whose anger is present every day.

13(12)   If a person will not repent,
he sharpens his sword.
He has bent his bow, made it ready;

14(13)   he has also prepared for him
weapons of death, his arrows,
which he has made into burning shafts.

15(14)   Look how the wicked is pregnant with evil;
he conceives trouble, gives birth to lies.

16(15)   He makes a pit, digs it deep,
and falls into the hole he made.

17(16)   His mischief will return onto his own head,
his violence will recoil onto his own skull.

18(17)   I thank *Adonai* for his righteousness
and sing praise to the name of *Adonai 'Elyon.*

8 $^{1(0)}$ For the leader. On the *gittit*. A psalm of David:

2(1)   *Adonai*! Our Lord! How glorious
is your name throughout the earth!
The fame of your majesty
spreads even above the heavens!

3(2)   From the mouths of babies and infants at the breast
you established strength because of your foes,
in order that you might silence
the enemy and the avenger.

4(3)   When I look at your heavens, the work of your fingers,
the moon and stars that you set in place —

5(4)   what are mere mortals, that you concern yourself with them;
humans, that you watch over them with such care?

6(5)   You made him but little lower than the angels,
you crowned him with glory and honor,

7(6)   you had him rule what your hands made,
you put everything under his feet —

8(7)   sheep and oxen, all of them,
also the animals in the wilds,

9(8)   the birds in the air, the fish in the sea,
whatever passes through the paths of the seas.

10(9)   *Adonai*! Our Lord! How glorious
is your name throughout the earth!

9 [1(0)] For the leader. On the death of Labben. A psalm of David:

[2(1)]   I give thanks to ADONAI with all my heart.
    I will tell about all your wonderful deeds.
[3(2)]   I will be glad and exult in you.
    I will sing praise to your name, '*Elyon.*

[4(3)]   When my enemies turn back,
    they stumble and perish before you.
[5(4)]   For you upheld my cause as just,
    sitting on the throne as the righteous judge.

[6(5)]   You rebuked the nations, destroyed the wicked,
    blotted out their name forever and ever.
[7(6)]   The enemy is finished, in ruins forever;
    you destroyed their cities; all memory of them is lost.

[8(7)]   But ADONAI is enthroned forever;
    he has set up his throne for judgment.
[9(8)]   He will judge the world in righteousness;
    he will judge the peoples fairly.

[10(9)]   ADONAI is a stronghold for the oppressed,
    a tower of strength in times of trouble.
[11(10)]   Those who know your name put their trust in you,
    for you have not abandoned those who seek you, ADONAI.

[12(11)]   Sing praises to ADONAI, who lives in Tziyon;
    proclaim his deeds among the peoples.
[13(12)]   For the avenger of blood remembers them,
    he does not ignore the cry of the afflicted:

[14(13)]   "Have mercy on me, ADONAI!
    See how I suffer from those who hate me;
    you raise me from the gates of death,
[15(14)]   so that I can proclaim all your praises
    at the gates of the daughter of Tziyon
    and rejoice in this deliverance of yours."

[16(15)]   The nations have drowned in the pit they dug,
    caught their own feet in the net they hid.
[17(16)]   ADONAI made himself known and executed judgment;
    the wicked are ensnared in the work of their own hands. (*Higgayon; Selah*)

[18(17)]   The wicked will return to Sh'ol,
    all the nations that forget God.

19(18)   For the poor will not always be forgotten
or the hope of the needy perish forever.

20(19)   Arise, ADONAI! Don't let mortals prevail!
Let the nations be judged in your presence.

21(20)   Strike them with terror, ADONAI!
Let the nations know they are only human.   *(Selah)*

10 ¹   Why, ADONAI, do you stand at a distance?
Why do you hide yourself in times of trouble?

2   The wicked in their arrogance hunt down the poor,
who get caught in the schemes they think up.

3   For the wicked boasts about his lusts;
he blesses greed and despises ADONAI.

4   Every scheme of the wicked in his arrogance [says],
"There is no God, [so] it won't be held against me."

5   His ways prosper at all times.
Your judgments are way up there,
so he takes no notice.
His adversaries? He scoffs at them all.

6   In his heart he thinks, "I will never be shaken;
I won't meet trouble, not now or ever."

7   His mouth is full of curses, deceit, oppression;
under his tongue, mischief and injustice.

8   He waits near settlements in ambush
and kills an innocent man in secret;
his eyes are on the hunt for the helpless.

9   Lurking unseen like a lion in his lair,
he lies in wait to pounce on the poor,
then seizes the poor and drags him off in his net.

10   Yes, he stoops, crouches down low;
and the helpless wretch falls into his clutches.

11   He says in his heart, "God forgets,
he hides his face, he will never see."

12   Arise, ADONAI! God, raise your hand!
Don't forget the humble!

13   Why does the wicked despise God
and say in his heart, "It won't be held against me"?

14   You have seen; for you look at mischief and grief,
so that you can take the matter in hand.
The helpless commits himself to you;
you help the fatherless.

15   Break the arm of the wicked!
As for the evil man,

search out his wickedness
until there is none left.

16 ADONAI is king forever and ever!
The nations have vanished from his land.
17 ADONAI, you have heard what the humble want;
you encourage them and listen to them,
18 to give justice to the fatherless and oppressed,
so that no one on earth will strike terror again.

11 $^{1(0)}$ For the leader. By David:

(1) In ADONAI I find refuge.
So how can you say to me,
"Flee like a bird to the mountains!
2 See how the wicked are drawing their bows
and setting their arrows on the string,
to shoot from the shadows at honest men.
3 If the foundations are destroyed,
what can the righteous do?"

4 ADONAI is in his holy temple.
ADONAI, his throne is in heaven.
His eyes see and test humankind.
5 ADONAI tests the righteous;
but he hates the wicked and the lover of violence.
6 He will rain hot coals down on the wicked,
fire, sulfur and scorching wind
will be what they get to drink.
7 For ADONAI is righteous;
he loves righteousness;
the upright will see his face.

12 $^{1(0)}$ For the leader. On *sh'minit* [low-pitched musical instruments?]. A psalm of David:

2(1) Help, ADONAI! For no one godly is left;
the faithful have vanished from humankind.
3(2) They all tell lies to each other,
flattering with their lips, but speaking from divided hearts.

4(3) May ADONAI cut off all flattering lips
and the tongue that speaks so proudly,
5(4) those who say, "By our tongues, we will prevail;
our lips are with us. Who can master us?"

11

6(5)   "Because the poor are oppressed,
    because the needy are groaning,
    I will now rise up," says ADONAI,
    "and grant security to those whom they scorn."

7(6)   The words of ADONAI are pure words,
    silver in a melting-pot set in the earth,
    refined and purified seven times over.

8(7)   You, ADONAI, protect us;
    guard us forever from this generation —

9(8)   the wicked strut about everywhere
    when vileness is held in general esteem.

13

1(0) For the leader. A psalm of David:

2(1)   How long, ADONAI?
    Will you forget me forever?
    How long will you hide your face from me?

3(2)   How long must I keep asking myself what to do,
    with sorrow in my heart every day?
    How long must my enemy dominate me?

4(3)   Look, and answer me, ADONAI my God!
    Give light to my eyes, or I will sleep the sleep of death.

5(4)   Then my enemy would say, "I was able to beat him";
    and my adversaries would rejoice at my downfall.

6(5)   But I trust in your grace,
    my heart rejoices as you bring me to safety.

(6)   I will sing to ADONAI, because he gives me
    even more than I need.

14

1(0) For the leader. By David:

(1)   Fools say in their hearts,
    "There is no God."
    They deal corruptly, their deeds are vile,
    not one does what is right.

2   From heaven ADONAI observes humankind
    to see if anyone has understanding,
    if anyone seeks God.

3   But all turn aside, all alike are corrupt;
    no one does what is right,
    not a single one.

⁴ Don't they ever learn,
all those evildoers,
who eat up my people as if eating bread
and never call on *Adonai*?
⁵ There they are, utterly terrified;
for God is with those who are righteous.
⁶ You may mock the plans of the poor,
but their refuge is *Adonai*.

⁷ How I wish Isra'el's salvation
would come out of Tziyon!
When *Adonai* restores his people's fortunes,
Ya'akov will rejoice, Isra'el will be glad!

15 ⁽⁰⁾ A psalm of David:

⁽¹⁾ *Adonai*, who can rest in your tent?
Who can live on your holy mountain?

² Those who live a blameless life,
who behave uprightly,
who speak truth from their hearts
³ and keep their tongues from slander;
who never do harm to others
or seek to discredit neighbors;
⁴ who look with scorn on the vile,
but honor those who fear *Adonai*;
who hold to an oath, no matter the cost;
⁵ who refuse usury when they lend money
and refuse a bribe to damage the innocent.

Those who do these things
never will be moved.

16 ⁽⁰⁾ *Mikhtam.* By David:

⁽¹⁾ Protect me, God,
for you are my refuge.
² I said to *Adonai*, "You are my Lord;
I have nothing good outside of you."
³ The holy people in the land are the ones
who are worthy of honor; all my pleasure is in them.

⁴ Those who run after another god
multiply their sorrows;

to such gods I will not offer
drink offerings of blood
or take their names on my lips.

5   A*DONAI*, my assigned portion, my cup:
you safeguard my share.
6   Pleasant places were measured out for me;
I am content with my heritage.

7   I bless A*DONAI*, my counselor;
at night my inmost being instructs me.
8   I always set A*DONAI* before me;
with him at my right hand, I can never be moved;
9   so my heart is glad, my glory rejoices,
and my body too rests in safety;
10   for you will not abandon me to Sh'ol,
you will not let your faithful one see the Abyss.
11   You make me know the path of life;
in your presence is unbounded joy,
in your right hand eternal delight.

17 ¹⁽⁰⁾ A prayer of David:

⁽¹⁾   Hear a just cause, A*DONAI*, heed my cry;
listen to my prayer from honest lips.
2   Let my vindication come from you,
let your eyes see what is right.

3   You probed my heart,
you visited me at night,
and you assayed me without finding evil thoughts
that should not pass my lips.
4   As for what others do, by words from your lips
I have kept myself from the ways of the violent;
5   my steps hold steadily to your paths,
my feet do not slip.

6   Now I call on you, God, for you will answer me.
Turn your ear to me, hear my words.
7   Show how wonderful is your grace,
savior of those who seek at your right hand
refuge from their foes.
8   Protect me like the pupil of your eye,
hide me in the shadow of your wings
9   from the wicked, who are assailing me,
from my deadly enemies, who are all around me.

10 They close their hearts to compassion;
they speak arrogantly with their mouths;
11 they track me down, they surround me;
they watch for a chance to bring me to the ground.
12 They are like lions eager to tear the prey,
like young lions crouching in ambush.

13 Arise, ADONAI, confront them! Bring them down!
With your sword deliver me from the wicked,
14 with your hand, ADONAI, from human beings,
from people whose portion in life is this world.
You fill their stomachs with your treasure,
their children will be satisfied too
and will leave their wealth to their little ones.

15 But my prayer, in righteousness, is to see your face;
on waking, may I be satisfied with a vision of you.

18 $^{1(1)}$ For the leader. By David the servant of ADONAI, who addressed the words of this song to ADONAI on the day when ADONAI delivered him from the power of all his enemies, including from the power of Sha'ul. ^{2} He said:

(1) "I love you, ADONAI, my strength!

3(2) "ADONAI is my Rock, my fortress and deliverer,
my God, my Rock, in whom I find shelter,
my shield, the power that saves me,
my stronghold.
4(3) I call on ADONAI, who is worthy of praise;
and I am saved from my enemies.

5(4) "For the cords of death surrounded me,
the floods of B'liya'al terrified me,
6(5) the ropes of Sh'ol were wrapped around me,
the snares of death lay there before me.
7(6) In my distress I called to ADONAI;
I cried out to my God.
Out of his temple he heard my voice;
my cry reached his ears.

8(7) "Then the earth quaked and shook,
the foundations of the mountains trembled.
They were shaken because he was angry.
9(8) Smoke arose in his nostrils;
out of his mouth came devouring fire;
sparks blazed forth from him.

10(9)	He lowered heaven and came down
	with thick darkness under his feet.
11(10)	He rode on a *keruv*; he flew,
	swooping down on the wings of the wind.
12(11)	He made darkness his hiding-place,
	his canopy thick clouds dark with water.
13(12)	From the brightness before him,
	there broke through his thick clouds
	hailstones and fiery coals.

14(13)	"*ADONAI* also thundered in heaven,
	Ha'Elyon sounded his voice —
	hailstones and fiery coals.
15(14)	He sent out arrows and scattered them,
	shot out lightning and routed them.
16(15)	The channels of water appeared,
	the foundations of the world were exposed
	at your rebuke, *ADONAI*,
	at the blast of breath from your nostrils.

17(16)	"He sent from on high, he took me
	and pulled me out of deep water;
18(17)	he rescued me from my powerful enemy,
	from those who hated me,
	for they were stronger than I.
19(18)	They came against me on my day of disaster,
	but *ADONAI* was my support.
20(19)	He brought me out to an open place;
	he rescued me, because he took pleasure in me.
21(20)	*ADONAI* rewarded me for my uprightness,
	he repaid me because my hands were clean.

22(21)	"For I have kept the ways of *ADONAI*,
	I have not done evil by leaving my God;
23(22)	for all his rulings were before me,
	I did not distance his regulations from me.
24(23)	I was pure-hearted with him
	and kept myself from my sin.

25(24)	"Hence *ADONAI* repaid me for my uprightness,
	according to the purity of my hands in his view.
26(25)	With the merciful, you are merciful;
	with a man who is sincere, you are sincere;
27(26)	with the pure, you are pure;
	but with the crooked you are cunning.
28(27)	People afflicted, you save;
	but haughty eyes, you humble.

29(28)   "For you, ADONAI, light my lamp;
        ADONAI, my God, lights up my darkness.
30(29)   With you I can run through a whole troop of men,
        with my God I can leap a wall.

31(30)   "As for God, his way is perfect,
        the word of ADONAI has been tested by fire;
        he shields all who take refuge in him.

32(31)   "For who is God but ADONAI?
        Who is a Rock but our God?

33(32)   "It is God who girds me with strength;
        he makes my way go straight.
34(33)   He makes me swift, sure-footed as a deer,
        and enables me to stand on my high places.
35(34)   He trains my hands for war
        until my arms can bend a bow of bronze;

36(35)   "You give me your shield, which is salvation,
        your right hand holds me up,
        your humility makes me great.
37(36)   You lengthen the steps I can take,
        yet my ankles do not turn.

38(37)   "I pursued my enemies and overtook them,
        without turning back until they were destroyed.
39(38)   I crushed them, so that they can't get up;
        they have fallen under my feet.

40(39)   "For you braced me with strength for the battle
        and bent down my adversaries beneath me.
41(40)   You made my enemies turn their backs in flight,
        and I destroyed those who hated me.

42(41)   "They cried out, but there was no one to help,
        even to ADONAI, but he didn't answer.
43(42)   I pulverized them like dust in the wind,
        threw them out like mud in the streets.

44(43)   "You also freed me from the quarrels of my people.
        You made me head of the nations;
        a people I did not know now serve me —
45(44)   the moment they hear of me, they obey me,
        foreigners come cringing to me.
46(45)   Foreigners lose heart
        as they come trembling from their fortresses.

47(46) "*ADONAI* is alive! Blessed is my Rock!
        Exalted be the God of my salvation,
48(47) the God who avenges me
        and subdues peoples under me.
49(48) He delivers me from my enemies.
        You lift me high above my enemies,
        you rescue me from violent men.

50(49) "So I give thanks to you, *ADONAI*, among the nations;
        I sing praises to your name.
51(50) Great salvation he gives to his king;
        he displays grace to his anointed,
        to David and his descendants forever."

19 ¹⁽⁰⁾ For the leader. A psalm of David:

2(1)   The heavens declare the glory of God,
        the dome of the sky speaks the work of his hands.
3(2)   Every day it utters speech,
        every night it reveals knowledge.
4(3)   Without speech, without a word,
        without their voices being heard,
5(4)   their line goes out through all the earth
        and their words to the end of the world.

        In them he places a tent for the sun,
6(5)   which comes out like a bridegroom from the bridal chamber,
        with delight like an athlete to run his race.
7(6)   It rises at one side of the sky,
        circles around to the other side,
        and nothing escapes its heat.

8(7)   The *Torah* of *ADONAI* is perfect,
        restoring the inner person.
        The instruction of *ADONAI* is sure,
        making wise the thoughtless.
9(8)   The precepts of *ADONAI* are right,
        rejoicing the heart.
        The *mitzvah* of *ADONAI* is pure,
        enlightening the eyes.
10(9)   The fear of *ADONAI* is clean,
        enduring forever.
        The rulings of *ADONAI* are true,
        they are righteous altogether,
11(10) more desirable than gold,
        than much fine gold,

also sweeter than honey
or drippings from the honeycomb.

12(11)   Through them your servant is warned;
in obeying them there is great reward.

13(12)   Who can discern unintentional sins?
Cleanse me from hidden faults.

14(13)   Also keep your servant from presumptuous sins,
so that they won't control me.
Then I will be blameless
and free of great offense.

15(14)   May the words of my mouth
and the thoughts of my heart
be acceptable in your presence,
ADONAI, my Rock and Redeemer.

20 1(0) For the leader. A psalm of David:

2(1)   May ADONAI answer you in times of distress,
may the name of the God of Ya'akov protect you.

3(2)   May he send you help from the sanctuary
and give you support from Tziyon.

4(3)   May he be reminded by all your grain offerings
and accept the fat of your burnt offerings.   (*Selah*)

5(4)   May he grant you your heart's desire
and bring all your plans to success.

6(5)   Then we will shout for joy at your victory
and fly our flags in the name of our God.
May ADONAI fulfill all your requests.

7(6)   Now I know that ADONAI
gives victory to his anointed one ——
he will answer him from his holy heaven
with mighty victories by his right hand.

8(7)   Some trust in chariots and some in horses,
but we praise the name of ADONAI our God.

9(8)   They will crumple and fall,
but we will arise and stand erect.

10(9)   Give victory, ADONAI!
Let the King answer us the day we call.

19

21 ¹⁽⁰⁾ For the leader. A psalm of David:

²⁽¹⁾   *Adonai*, the king finds joy in your strength;
    what great joy he displays in your victory!
³⁽²⁾   You give him his heart's desire;
    you don't refuse the prayer from his lips.   *(Selah)*

⁴⁽³⁾   For you come to meet him with the best blessings,
    you place a crown of fine gold on his head.
⁵⁽⁴⁾   He asks you for life; you give it to him,
    years and years forever and ever.

⁶⁽⁵⁾   Your victory brings him great glory;
    you confer on him splendor and honor.
⁷⁽⁶⁾   For you bestow on him everlasting blessings,
    you make him glad with the joy of your presence.
⁸⁽⁷⁾   For the king puts his trust in *Adonai*,
    in the grace of *'Elyon*; he will not be moved.

⁹⁽⁸⁾   Your hand will find all your enemies;
    your right hand will overtake those who hate you.
¹⁰⁽⁹⁾   At your appearing,
    you will make them like a fiery furnace.
    Adonai will swallow them up in his anger;
    fire will consume them.
¹¹⁽¹⁰⁾   You will destroy from the earth their descendants,
    rid humankind of their posterity;
¹²⁽¹¹⁾   for they intended evil against you;
    but despite their scheme, they won't succeed.
¹³⁽¹²⁾   For you will make them turn their back
    by aiming your bow at their faces.

¹⁴⁽¹³⁾   Arise, *Adonai*, in your strength;
    and we will sing and praise your power.

22 ¹⁽⁰⁾ For the leader. Set to "Sunrise." A psalm of David:

²⁽¹⁾   My God! My God!
    Why have you abandoned me?
    Why so far from helping me,
    so far from my anguished cries?

³⁽²⁾   My God, by day I call to you,
    but you don't answer;
    likewise at night,
    but I get no relief.

4(3)   Nevertheless, you are holy,
        enthroned on the praises of Isra'el.
5(4)   In you our ancestors put their trust;
        they trusted, and you rescued them.
6(5)   They cried to you and escaped;
        they trusted in you and were not disappointed.

7(6)   But I am a worm, not a man,
        scorned by everyone, despised by the people.
8(7)   All who see me jeer at me;
        they sneer and shake their heads:
9(8)   "He committed himself to ADONAI,
        so let him rescue him!
        Let him set him free
        if he takes such delight in him!"

10(9)   But you are the one who took me from the womb,
        you made me trust when I was on my mother's breasts.
11(10)   Since my birth I've been thrown on you;
        you are my God from my mother's womb.
12(11)   Don't stay far from me, for trouble is near;
        and there is no one to help.
13(12)   Many bulls surround me,
        wild bulls of Bashan close in on me.
14(13)   They open their mouths wide against me,
        like ravening, roaring lions.
15(14)   I am poured out like water;
        all my bones are out of joint;
        my heart has become like wax —
        it melts inside me;
16(15)   my mouth is as dry as a fragment of a pot,
        my tongue sticks to my palate;
        you lay me down in the dust of death.
17(16)   Dogs are all around me,
        a pack of villains closes in on me
        like a lion [at] my hands and feet.*

18(17)   I can count every one of my bones,
        while they gaze at me and gloat.
19(18)   They divide my garments among themselves;
        for my clothing they throw dice.

20(19)   But you, ADONAI, don't stay far away!
        My strength, come quickly to help me!
21(20)   Rescue me from the sword,

---

*Or: "They pierced my hands and feet." See Introduction, Section VIII, paragraph 6, and Section XIV, footnote 70.

22(21)
my life from the power of the dogs.
Save me from the lion's mouth!

23(22)
You have answered me from the wild bulls' horns.
I will proclaim your name to my kinsmen;
right there in the assembly I will praise you:

24(23)
"You who fear ADONAI, praise him!
All descendants of Ya'akov, glorify him!
All descendants of Isra'el, stand in awe of him!

25(24)
For he has not despised or abhorred
the poverty of the poor;
he did not hide his face from him
but listened to his cry."

26(25)
Because of you
I give praise in the great assembly;
I will fulfill my vows
in the sight of those who fear him.

27(26)
The poor will eat and be satisfied;
those who seek ADONAI will praise him;
Your hearts will enjoy life forever.

28(27)
All the ends of the earth
will remember and turn to ADONAI;
all the clans of the nations
will worship in your presence.

29(28)
For the kingdom belongs to ADONAI,
and he rules the nations.

30(29)
All who prosper on the earth
will eat and worship;
all who go down to the dust
will kneel before him,
including him who can't keep himself alive.

31(30)
A descendant will serve him;
the next generation will be told of *Adonai*.

32(31)
They will come and proclaim
his righteousness
to a people yet unborn,
that he is the one who did it.

23 ¹⁽⁰⁾ A psalm of David:

(1)
ADONAI is my shepherd; I lack nothing.

2
He has me lie down in grassy pastures,
he leads me by quiet water,

3
he restores my inner person.

22

He guides me in right paths
for the sake of his own name.
4   Even if I pass through death-dark ravines,
I will fear no disaster; for you are with me;
your rod and staff reassure me.

5   You prepare a table for me,
even as my enemies watch;
you anoint my head with oil
from an overflowing cup.

6   Goodness and grace will pursue me
every day of my life;
and I will live in the house of ADONAI
for years and years to come.

24 ⁽⁰⁾ By David. A psalm:

(1) The earth is ADONAI's, with all that is in it,
the world and those who live there;
2   for he set its foundations on the seas
and established it on the rivers.

3   Who may go up to the mountain of ADONAI?
Who can stand in his holy place?
4   Those with clean hands and pure hearts,
who don't make vanities the purpose of their lives
or swear oaths just to deceive.
5   They will receive a blessing from ADONAI
and justice from God, who saves them.
6   Such is the character of those who seek him,
of Ya'akov, who seeks your face.   (*Selah*)

7   Lift up your heads, you gates!
Lift them up, everlasting doors,
so that the glorious king can enter!
8   Who is he, this glorious king?
ADONAI, strong and mighty,
ADONAI, mighty in battle.

9   Lift up your heads, you gates!
Lift them up, everlasting doors,
so that the glorious king can enter!
10   Who is he, this glorious king?
ADONAI-*Tzva'ot* —
he is the glorious king.   (*Selah*)

25 [1(0)] By David:

[(1)] I lift my inner being to you, Adonai;
[2] I trust you, my God.
Don't let me be disgraced,
don't let my enemies gloat over me.
[3] No one waiting for you will be disgraced;
disgrace awaits those who break faith for no reason.

[4] Make me know your ways, Adonai,
teach me your paths.
[5] Guide me in your truth, and teach me;
for you are the God who saves me,
my hope is in you all day long.
[6] Remember your compassion and grace, Adonai;
for these are ages old.
[7] Don't remember my youthful sins or transgressions;
but remember me according to your grace
for the sake of your goodness, Adonai.

[8] Adonai is good, and he is fair;
this is why he teaches sinners the way [to live],
[9] leads the humble to do what is right
and teaches the humble [to live] his way.
[10] All Adonai's paths are grace and truth
to those who keep his covenant and instructions.
[11] For the sake of your name, Adonai,
forgive my wickedness, great though it is.

[12] Who is the person who fears Adonai?
He will teach him the way to choose.
[13] He will remain prosperous,
and his descendants will inherit the land.
[14] Adonai relates intimately with those who fear him;
he makes them know his covenant.

[15] My eyes are always directed toward Adonai,
for he will free my feet from the net.
[16] Turn to me, and show me your favor;
for I am alone and oppressed.
[17] The troubles of my heart are growing and growing;
bring me out of my distress.
[18] See my affliction and suffering,
and take all my sins away.

[19] Consider my enemies, how many there are
and how cruelly they hate me.

20 Protect me and rescue me;
    don't let me be disgraced,
    for I take refuge in you.
21 Let integrity and uprightness preserve me,
    because my hope is in you.

22 God! Redeem Isra'el
    from all their troubles!

26 ¹⁽⁰⁾ By David:

(1) Vindicate me, ADONAI,
     for I have lived a blameless life;
     unwaveringly I trust in ADONAI.
2   Examine me, ADONAI, test me,
     search my mind and heart.
3   For your grace is there before my eyes,
     and I live my life by your truth.
4   I have not sat with worthless folks,
     I won't consort with hypocrites,
5   I hate the company of evildoers,
     I will not sit with the wicked.

6   I will wash my hands in innocence
     and walk around your altar, ADONAI,
7   lifting my voice in thanks
     and proclaiming all your wonders.
8   ADONAI, I love the house where you live,
     the place where your glory abides.

9   Don't include me with sinners
     or my life with the bloodthirsty.
10   In their hands are evil schemes;
     their right hands are full of bribes.
11   As for me, I will live a blameless life.
     Redeem me and show me favor.
12   My feet are planted on level ground;
     in the assemblies I will bless ADONAI.

27 ¹⁽⁰⁾ By David:

(1) ADONAI is my light and salvation;
     whom do I need to fear?
     ADONAI is the stronghold of my life;
     of whom should I be afraid?

2 When evildoers assailed me
to devour my flesh,
my adversaries and foes,
they stumbled and fell.
3 If an army encamps against me,
my heart will not fear;
if war breaks out against me,
even then I will keep trusting.

4 Just one thing have I asked of ADONAI;
only this will I seek:
to live in the house of ADONAI
all the days of my life,
to see the beauty of ADONAI
and visit in his temple.
5 For he will conceal me in his shelter
on the day of trouble,
he will hide me in the folds of his tent,
he will set me high on a rock.
6 Then my head will be lifted up
above my surrounding foes,
and I will offer in his tent
sacrifices with shouts of joy;
I will sing, sing praises to ADONAI.

7 Listen, ADONAI, to my voice when I cry;
show favor to me; and answer me.
8 "My heart said of you, 'Seek my face.'"
Your face, ADONAI, I will seek.
9 Do not hide your face from me,
don't turn your servant away in anger.
You are my help; don't abandon me;
don't leave me, God my savior.
10 Even though my father and mother have left me,
ADONAI will care for me.
11 Teach me your way, ADONAI;
lead me on a level path
because of my enemies —
12 don't give me up to the whims of my foes;
for false witnesses have risen against me,
also those who are breathing violence.

13 If I hadn't believed that I would see
ADONAI's goodness in the land of the living, . . .
14 Put your hope in ADONAI, be strong,
and let your heart take courage!
Yes, put your hope in ADONAI!

28 ¹⁽¹⁾ By David:

⁽¹⁾ ADONAI, I am calling to you;
my Rock, don't be deaf to my cry.
For if you answer me with silence,
I will be like those who fall in a pit.

² Hear the sound of my prayers
when I cry to you,
when I lift my hands
toward your holy sanctuary.

³ Don't drag me off with the wicked,
with those whose deeds are evil;
they speak words of peace to their fellowmen,
but evil is in their hearts.

⁴ Pay them back for their deeds,
as befits their evil acts;
repay them for what they have done,
give them what they deserve.

⁵ For they don't understand the deeds of ADONAI
or what he has done.
He will break them down;
he will not build them up.

⁶ Blessed be ADONAI,
for he heard my voice as I prayed for mercy.

⁷ ADONAI is my strength and shield;
in him my heart trusted, and I have been helped.
Therefore my heart is filled with joy,
and I will sing praises to him.

⁸ ADONAI is strength for [his people],
a stronghold of salvation to his anointed.

⁹ Save your people! Bless your heritage!
Shepherd them, and carry them forever!

29 ¹⁽¹⁾ A psalm of David:

⁽¹⁾ Give ADONAI his due, you who are godly;
give ADONAI his due of glory and strength;

² give ADONAI the glory due his name;
worship ADONAI in holy splendor.

³ The voice of ADONAI is over the waters;
the God of glory thunders,
ADONAI over rushing waters,

⁴ the voice of ADONAI in power,
the voice of ADONAI in splendor.

⁵ The voice of ADONAI cracks the cedars;
ADONAI splinters the cedars of the L'vanon
⁶ and makes the L'vanon skip like a calf,
Siryon like a young wild ox.

⁷ The voice of ADONAI flashes fiery flames;
⁸ the voice of ADONAI rocks the desert,
ADONAI convulses the Kadesh Desert.
⁹ The voice of ADONAI causes deer to give birth
and strips the forests bare —
while in his temple, all cry, "Glory!"
¹⁰ ADONAI sits enthroned above the flood!
ADONAI sits enthroned as king forever!
¹¹ May ADONAI give strength to his people!
May ADONAI bless his people with *shalom*!

30 ¹⁽⁰⁾ A psalm. A song for the dedication of the house. By David:

²⁽¹⁾ I will exalt you, ADONAI, because you drew me up;
you didn't let my enemies rejoice over me.
³⁽²⁾ ADONAI my God, I cried out to you,
and you provided healing for me.
⁴⁽³⁾ ADONAI, you lifted me up from Sh'ol;
you kept me alive when I was sinking into a pit.

⁵⁽⁴⁾ Sing praise to ADONAI, you faithful of his;
and give thanks on recalling his holiness.
⁶⁽⁵⁾ For his anger is momentary,
but his favor lasts a lifetime.
Tears may linger for the night,
but with dawn come cries of joy.

⁷⁽⁶⁾ Once I was prosperous and used to say
that nothing could ever shake me —
⁸⁽⁷⁾ when you showed me favor, ADONAI,
I was firm as a mighty mountain.
But when you hid your face,
I was struck with terror.

⁹⁽⁸⁾ I called to you, ADONAI;
to ADONAI I pleaded for mercy:
¹⁰⁽⁹⁾ "What advantage is there in my death,
in my going down to the pit?

11(10)
Can the dust praise you?
Can it proclaim your truth?
Hear me, ADONAI, and show me your favor!
ADONAI, be my helper!"

12(11)
You turned my mourning into dancing!
You removed my sackcloth and clothed me with joy,

13(12)
so that my well-being can praise you and not be silent;
ADONAI my God, I will thank you forever!

31¹⁽⁰⁾ For the leader. A psalm of David:

2(1)
In you, ADONAI, I take refuge;
let me never be put to shame;
in your justice, save me!

3(2)
Turn your ear toward me,
come quickly to my rescue,
be for me a rock of strength,
a fortress to keep me safe.

4(3)
Since you are my rock and fortress,
lead me and guide me for your name's sake.

5(4)
Free me from the net they have hidden to catch me,
because you are my strength.

6(5)
Into your hand I commit my spirit;
you will redeem me, ADONAI, God of truth.

7(6)
I hate those who serve worthless idols;
as for me, I trust in ADONAI.

8(7)
I will rejoice and be glad in your grace,
for you see my affliction,
you know how distressed I am.

9(8)
You did not hand me over to the enemy;
you set my feet where I can move freely.

10(9)
Show me favor, ADONAI, for I am in trouble.
My eyes grow dim with anger,
my soul and body as well.

11(10)
For my life is worn out with sorrow
and my years with sighing;
my strength gives out under my guilt,
and my bones are wasting away.

12(11)
I am scorned by all my adversaries,
and even more by my neighbors;
even to acquaintances
I am an object of fear —

when they see me in the street,
they turn away from me.
13(12) Like a dead man, I have passed from their minds;
I have become like a broken pot.
14(13) All I hear is whispering,
terror is all around me;
they plot together against me,
scheming to take my life.

15(14) But I, I trust in you, ADONAI;
I say, "You are my God."
16(15) My times are in your hand;
rescue me from my enemies' power,
from those who persecute me.

17(16) Make your face shine on your servant;
in your grace, save me.
18(17) ADONAI, don't let me be put to shame,
for I have called on you;
let the wicked be put to shame,
let them be silenced in Sh'ol.
19(18) May lying lips be struck dumb,
that speak insolently against the righteous
with such pride and contempt.

20(19) But oh, how great is your goodness,
which you have stored up for those who fear you,
which you do for those who take refuge in you,
before people's very eyes!
21(20) In the shelter of your presence
you hide them from human plots,
you conceal them in your shelter,
safe from contentious tongues.

22(21) Blessed be ADONAI!
For he has shown me his amazing grace
when I was in a city under siege.
23(22) As for me, in my alarm I said,
"I have been cut off from your sight!"
Nevertheless, you heard my pleas
when I cried out to you.

24(23) Love ADONAI, you faithful of his.
ADONAI preserves the loyal,
but the proud he repays in full.
25(24) Be strong, and fill your hearts with courage,
all of you who hope in ADONAI.

32 ¹⁽⁰⁾ By David. A *maskil*:

⁽¹⁾   How blessed are those whose offense is forgiven,
       those whose sin is covered!
²   How blessed those to whom ADONAI imputes no guilt,
       in whose spirit is no deceit!

³   When I kept silent, my bones wasted away
       because of my groaning all day long;
⁴   day and night your hand was heavy on me;
       the sap in me dried up as in a summer drought.   (*Selah*)

⁵   When I acknowledged my sin to you,
       when I stopped concealing my guilt,
       and said, "I will confess my offenses to ADONAI";
       then you, you forgave the guilt of my sin.   (*Selah*)

⁶   This is what everyone faithful should pray
       at a time when you can be found.
       Then, when the floodwaters are raging,
       they will not reach to him.

⁷   You are a hiding-place for me,
       you will keep me from distress;
       you will surround me
       with songs of deliverance.   (*Selah*)

⁸   "I will instruct and teach you
       in this way that you are to go;
       I will give you counsel;
       my eyes will be watching you."

⁹   Don't be like a horse or mule
       that has no understanding,
       that has to be curbed with bit and bridle,
       or else it won't come near you.

¹⁰   Many are the torments of the wicked,
       but grace surrounds those who trust in ADONAI.
¹¹   Be glad in ADONAI; rejoice, you righteous!
       Shout for joy, all you upright in heart!

33 ¹   Rejoice in ADONAI, you righteous!
       Praise is well-suited to the upright.
²   Give thanks to ADONAI with the lyre,
       sing praises to him with a ten-stringed harp.

3 Sing to him a new song,
   make music at your best among shouts of joy.
4 For the word of *Adonai* is true,
   and all his work is trustworthy.
5 He loves righteousness and justice;
   the earth is full of the grace of *Adonai*.

6 By the word of *Adonai* the heavens were made,
   and their whole host by a breath from his mouth.
7 He collects the sea waters together in a heap;
   he puts the deeps in storehouses.

8 Let all the earth fear *Adonai*!
   Let all living in the world stand in awe of him.
9 For he spoke, and there it was;
   he commanded, and there it stood.

10 *Adonai* brings to nothing the plans of nations,
   he foils the plans of the peoples.
11 But the counsel of *Adonai* stands forever,
   his heart's plans are for all generations.
12 How blessed is the nation whose God is *Adonai*,
   the people he chose as his heritage!

13 *Adonai* looks out from heaven;
   he sees every human being;
14 from the place where he lives
   he watches everyone living on earth,
15 he who fashioned the hearts of them all
   and understands all they do.

16 A king is not saved by the size of his army,
   a strong man not delivered by his great strength.
17 To rely on a horse for safety is vain,
   nor does its great power assure escape.

18 But *Adonai*'s eyes watch over those who fear him,
   over those who wait for his grace
19 to rescue them from death
   and keep them alive in famine.

20 We are waiting for *Adonai*;
   he is our help and shield.
21 For in him our hearts rejoice,
   because we trust in his holy name.
22 May your mercy, *Adonai*, be over us,
   because we put our hope in you.

34 [1(0)] By David, when he pretended to be insane before Avimelekh, who then drove him away; so he left:

[2(1)] I will bless *Adonai* at all times;
his praise will always be in my mouth.
[3(2)] When I boast, it will be about *Adonai*;
the humble will hear of it and be glad.

[4(3)] Proclaim with me the greatness of *Adonai*;
let us exalt his name together.
[5(4)] I sought *Adonai*, and he answered me;
he rescued me from everything I feared.

[6(5)] They looked to him and grew radiant;
their faces will never blush for shame.
[7(6)] This poor man cried; *Adonai* heard
and saved him from all his troubles.
[8(7)] The angel of *Adonai*, who encamps
around those who fear him, delivers them.

[9(8)] Taste, and see that *Adonai* is good.
How blessed are those who take refuge in him!
[10(9)] Fear *Adonai*, you holy ones of his,
for those who fear him lack nothing.
[11(10)] Young lions can be needy, they can go hungry,
but those who seek *Adonai* lack nothing good.

[12(11)] Come, children, listen to me;
I will teach you the fear of *Adonai*.
[13(12)] Which of you takes pleasure in living?
Who wants a long life to see good things?
[14(13)] [If you do,] keep your tongue from evil
and your lips from deceiving talk;
[15(14)] turn from evil, and do good;
seek peace, go after it!

[16(15)] The eyes of *Adonai* watch over the righteous,
and his ears are open to their cry.
[17(16)] But the face of *Adonai* opposes those who do evil,
to cut off all memory of them from the earth.

[18(17)] [The righteous] cried out, and *Adonai* heard,
and he saved them from all their troubles.
[19(18)] *Adonai* is near those with broken hearts;
he saves those whose spirit is crushed.
[20(19)] The righteous person suffers many evils,
but *Adonai* rescues him out of them all.

21(20)	He protects all his bones;
	not one of them gets broken.

22(21)	Evil will kill the wicked,
	and those who hate the righteous will be condemned.
23(22)	But ADONAI redeems his servants;
	no one who takes refuge in him will be condemned.

35 ¹⁽⁰⁾ By David:

(1)	ADONAI, oppose those who oppose me;
	fight against those who fight against me.
2	Grasp your shield and protective gear,
	and rise to my defense.
3	Brandish spear and battle-axe
	against my pursuers;
	let me hear you say,
	"I am your salvation."

4	May those who seek my life
	be disgraced and put to confusion;
	may those who are plotting harm for me
	be repulsed and put to shame.
5	May they be like chaff before the wind,
	with the angel of ADONAI to drive them on.
6	May their way be dark and slippery,
	with the angel of ADONAI to pursue them.
7	For unprovoked, they hid their net over a pit;
	unprovoked, they dug it for me.
8	May destruction come over him unawares.
	May the net he concealed catch himself;
	may he fall into it and be destroyed.

9	Then I will be joyful in ADONAI,
	I will rejoice in his salvation.
10	All my bones will say,
	"Who is like you?
	Who can rescue the weak
	from those stronger than they,
	the poor and needy
	from those who exploit them?"

11	Malicious witnesses come forward,
	asking me things about which I know nothing.
12	They repay me evil for good;
	it makes me feel desolate as a parent bereaved.

13 But I, when they were ill, wore sackcloth;
    I put myself out and fasted;
    I can pray that what I prayed for them
    might also happen to me.
14 I behaved as I would for my friend or my brother;
    I bent down in sorrow as if mourning my mother.

15 But when I stumble, they gather in glee;
    they gather against me and strike me unawares;
    they tear me apart unceasingly.
16 With ungodly mocking and grimacing,
    they grind their teeth at me.
17 *Adonai*, how much longer will you look on?
    Rescue me from their assaults,
    save the one life I have from the lions!

18 I will give you thanks in the great assembly,
    I will give you praise among huge crowds of people.
19 Don't let those who are wrongfully my enemies
    gloat over me;
    and those who hate me unprovoked —
    don't let them smirk at me.

20 For they don't speak words of peace
    but devise ways to deceive
    the peaceful of the land.
21 They shout to accuse me, "Aha! Aha!
    we saw you with our own eyes!"
22 You saw them, *Adonai*; don't stay silent.
    Adonai, don't stay far away from me.

23 Wake up! Get up, my God, my Lord!
    Defend me and my cause!
24 Give judgment for me, *Adonai*, my God,
    as your righteousness demands.

    Don't let them gloat over me.
25 Don't let them say to themselves,
    "Aha! We got what we wanted!"
    or say, "We swallowed them up!"
26 May those who gloat over my distress
    be disgraced and humiliated.
    May those who aggrandize themselves at my expense
    be covered with shame and confusion.

27 But may those who delight in my righteousness
    shout for joy and be glad!

Let them say always, "How great is ADONAI,
who delights in the peace of his servant!"
28   Then my tongue will tell of your righteousness
and praise you all day long.

36 ¹⁽⁰⁾ For the leader. By David, the servant of ADONAI:

2(1)   Crime speaks to the wicked.
I perceive this in my heart;
before his eyes there is no fear
of God.
3(2)   For, the way he sees it,
crime makes his life easy —
that is, until his wrongs are discovered;
then, he is hated.
4(3)   His words are wrong and deceitful;
he has stopped being wise and doing good.
5(4)   He devises trouble as he lies in bed;
so set is he on his own bad way
that he doesn't hate evil.

6(5)   ADONAI, in the heavens is your grace;
your faithfulness reaches to the skies.
7(6)   Your righteousness is like the mountains of God,
your judgments are like the great deep.
You save man and beast, ADONAI.
8(7)   How precious, God, is your grace!
People take refuge in the shadow of your wings,
9(8)   they feast on the rich bounty of your house,
and you have them drink from the stream of your delights.
10(9)   For with you is the fountain of life;
in your light we see light.
11(10)   Continue your grace to those who know you
and your righteousness to the upright in heart.
12(11)   Don't let the foot of the proud tread on me
or the hands of the wicked drive me away.
13(12)   There they lie fallen, those evildoers,
flung down and unable to rise.

37 ¹⁽⁰⁾ By David:

(1)   Don't be upset by evildoers
or envious of those who do wrong,
2   for soon they will wither like grass
and fade like the green in the fields.

36

3 Trust in *Adonai*, and do good;
   settle in the land, and feed on faithfulness.
4 Then you will delight yourself in *Adonai*,
   and he will give you your heart's desire.

5 Commit your way to *Adonai*;
   trust in him, and he will act.
6 He will make your vindication shine forth like light,
   the justice of your cause like the noonday sun.

7 Be still before *Adonai*;
   wait patiently till he comes.
   Don't be upset by those whose way
   succeeds because of their wicked plans.
8 Stop being angry, put aside rage,
   and don't be upset — it leads to evil.

9 For evildoers will be cut off,
   but those hoping in *Adonai* will inherit the land.
10 Soon the wicked will be no more;
   you will look for his place, and he won't be there.
11 But the meek will inherit the land
   and delight themselves in abundant peace.

12 The wicked plots against the righteous
   and grinds his teeth at him;
13 but *Adonai* laughs at the wicked,
   knowing his day will come.
14 The wicked have unsheathed their swords,
   they have strung their bows
   to bring down the poor and needy,
   to slaughter those whose way is upright.
15 But their swords will pierce their own hearts,
   and their bows will be broken.

16 Better the little that the righteous has
   than the wealth of all the wicked.
17 For the arms of the wicked will be broken,
   but *Adonai* upholds the righteous.
18 *Adonai* knows what the wholehearted suffer,
   but their inheritance lasts forever.
19 They will not be distressed when times are hard;
   when famine comes, they will have plenty.

20 For the wicked will perish;
   Adonai's enemies will be like sheep fat,
   ending up as smoke, finished.

21 The wicked borrows and doesn't repay,
but the righteous is generous and gives.
22 For those blessed by [ADONAI] will inherit the land,
but those cursed by him will be cut off.

23 ADONAI directs a person's steps,
and he delights in his way.
24 He may stumble, but he won't fall headlong,
for ADONAI holds him by the hand.

25 I have been young; now I am old;
yet not once have I seen the righteous abandoned
or his descendants begging for bread.
26 All day long he is generous and lends,
and his descendants are blessed.

27 If you turn from evil and do good,
you will live safely forever.
28 For ADONAI loves justice
and will not abandon his faithful;
they are preserved forever.
But the descendants of the wicked will be cut off.

29 The righteous will inherit the land
and live in it forever.
30 The mouth of the righteous articulates wisdom,
his tongue speaks justice.
31 The *Torah* of his God is in his heart;
his footsteps do not falter.

32 The wicked keeps his eye on the righteous,
seeking a chance to kill him.
33 But ADONAI will not leave him in his power
or let him be condemned when judged.
34 Put your hope in ADONAI, keep to his way,
and he will raise you up to inherit the land.

When the wicked are cut off, you will see it.
35 I have seen a wicked man wielding great power,
flourishing like a shade tree in its native soil.
36 But I passed by again, and he was no longer there;
I looked for him, but he could not be found.

37 Observe the pure person, consider the upright;
for the peaceful person will have posterity.
38 But transgressors will all be destroyed;
the posterity of the wicked will be cut off.

³⁹ *Adonai* is the one who saves the righteous;
he is their stronghold in time of trouble.
⁴⁰ *Adonai* helps them and rescues them,
rescues them from the wicked and saves them;
because they take refuge in him.

38 ¹⁽⁰⁾ A psalm of David, serving as a reminder:

²⁽¹⁾ *Adonai*, don't rebuke me when you are angry
or discipline me when you are enraged,
³⁽²⁾ for your arrows penetrate me deeply,
and your hand is pressing me down.

⁴⁽³⁾ Your indignation left no part of me intact;
my sin made my whole body sick;
⁵⁽⁴⁾ for my iniquities loom high over my head
as a heavy burden, too heavy for me.

⁶⁽⁵⁾ I have stinking, festering wounds
because of my foolishness.
⁷⁽⁶⁾ I am bent down, prostrate completely;
I go about mourning all day long.

⁸⁽⁷⁾ For my insides burn with fever,
and my whole body is sick.
⁹⁽⁸⁾ I am numb, completely crushed;
my anguished heart makes me groan aloud.

¹⁰⁽⁹⁾ *Adonai*, all my longing is known to you;
my sighing is not hidden from you.
¹¹⁽¹⁰⁾ My heart is throbbing, my strength is gone,
and the light in my eyes has left me.

¹²⁽¹¹⁾ My friends and companions shun my disease;
even the closest keep their distance.
¹³⁽¹²⁾ Those seeking my life lay snares for me,
those seeking to harm me speak of disaster
and think up deceptions all day long.

¹⁴⁽¹³⁾ But I'm like a deaf man — I don't hear it;
and, like a mute, I don't say a word.
¹⁵⁽¹⁴⁾ Yes, I've become like a man who doesn't hear
and in whose mouth are no defenses.

¹⁶⁽¹⁵⁾ For it is in you, *Adonai*, that I hope.
You will answer, *Adonai* my God.

17(16)   I said, "Don't let them gloat over me
          or boast against me when my foot slips."

18(17)   For I am about to fall,
          and my pain is always with me.
19(18)   I acknowledge my guilt,
          I am anxious because of my sin.

20(19)   But my enemies are alive and well,
          those who wrongfully hate me increase their numbers;
21(20)   and, since they repay good with evil,
          they oppose me because I pursue good.

22(21)   Don't abandon me, ADONAI!
          My God, don't be far from me!
23(22)   Come quickly to help me,
          Adonai, my salvation!

39 [1(0)] For the leader. Set in the style of Y'dutun. A psalm of David:

2(1)   I said, "I will watch how I behave,
          so that I won't sin with my tongue;
          I will put a muzzle on my mouth
          whenever the wicked confront me."

3(2)   I was silent, said nothing, not even good;
          but my pain kept being stirred up.
4(3)   My heart grew hot within me;
          whenever I thought of it, the fire burned.
          Then, [at last,] I let my tongue speak:

5(4)   "Make me grasp, ADONAI, what my end must be,
          what it means that my days are numbered;
          let me know what a transient creature I am.
6(5)   You have made my days like handbreadths;
          for you, the length of my life is like nothing."

          Yes, everyone, no matter how firmly he stands,
          is merely a puff of wind.   (*Selah*)
7(6)   Humans go about like shadows;
          their turmoil is all for nothing.
          They accumulate wealth, not knowing
          who will enjoy its benefits.

8(7)   Now, *Adonai*, what am I waiting for?
          You are my only hope.

9(8) Rescue me from all my transgressions;
don't make me the butt of fools.
10(9) I am silent, I keep my mouth shut,
because it is you who have done it.

11(10) Stop raining blows on me;
the pounding of your fist is wearing me down.
12(11) With rebukes you discipline people for their guilt;
like a moth, you destroy what makes them attractive;
yes, everyone is merely a puff of wind.   (*Selah*)

13(12) Hear my prayer, ADONAI, listen to my cry,
don't be deaf to my weeping;
for with you, I am just a traveler
passing through, like all my ancestors.
14(13) Turn your gaze from me, so I can smile again
before I depart and cease to exist.

40 1(0) For the leader. A psalm of David:

2(1) I waited patiently for ADONAI,
till he turned toward me and heard my cry.
3(2) He brought me up from the roaring pit,
up from the muddy ooze,
and set my feet on a rock,
making my footing firm.
4(3) He put a new song in my mouth,
a song of praise to our God.
Many will look on in awe
and put their trust in ADONAI.

5(4) How blessed the man who trusts in ADONAI
and does not look to the arrogant
or to those who rely on things that are false.

6(5) How much you have done, ADONAI my God!
Your wonders and your thoughts toward us —
none can compare with you!
I would proclaim them, I would speak about them;
but there's too much to tell!

7(6) Sacrifices and grain offerings you don't want;
burnt offerings and sin offerings you don't demand.
Instead, you have given me open ears;
8(7) so then I said, "Here I am! I'm coming!
In the scroll of a book it is written about me.

41

9(8)	Doing your will, my God, is my joy;
	your *Torah* is in my inmost being.
10(9)	I have proclaimed what is right in the great assembly;
	I did not restrain my lips, ADONAI, as you know.
11(10)	I did not hide your righteousness in my heart
	but declared your faithfulness and salvation;
	I did not conceal your grace and truth
	from the great assembly."

12(11)	ADONAI, don't withhold your mercy from me.
	Let your grace and truth preserve me always.
13(12)	For numberless evils surround me;
	my iniquities engulf me — I can't even see;
	there are more of them than hairs on my head,
	so that my courage fails me.
14(13)	Be pleased, ADONAI, to rescue me!
	ADONAI, hurry and help me!
15(14)	May those who seek to sweep me away
	be disgraced and humiliated together.
	May those who take pleasure in doing me harm
	be turned back and put to confusion.
16(15)	May those who jeer at me, "Aha! Aha!"
	be aghast because of their shame.

17(16)	But may all those who seek you
	be glad and take joy in you.
	May those who love your salvation say always,
	"ADONAI is great and glorious!"

18(17)	But I am poor and needy;
	may *Adonai* think of me.
	You are my helper and rescuer;
	my God, don't delay!

41 ¹⁽⁰⁾ For the leader. A psalm of David:

2(1)	How blessed are those who care for the poor!
	When calamity comes, ADONAI will save them.
3(2)	ADONAI will preserve them, keep them alive,
	and make them happy in the land.
	You will not hand them over
	to the whims of their enemies.
4(3)	ADONAI sustains them on their sickbed;
	when they lie ill, you make them recover.
5(4)	I said, "ADONAI, have pity on me!
	Heal me, for I have sinned against you!"

6(5) My enemies say the worst about me:
      "When will he die and his name disappear?"
7(6) When they come to see me they speak insincerely,
      their hearts meanwhile gathering falsehoods;
      then they go out and spread bad reports.
8(7) All who hate me whisper together against me,
      imagining the worst about me.
9(8) "A fatal disease has attached itself to him;
      now that he lies ill, he will never get up."
10(9) Even my close friend, on whom I relied,
      who shared my table, has turned against me.

11(10) But you, ADONAI, have pity on me,
      put me on my feet, so I can pay them back.
12(11) I will know you are pleased with me
      if my enemy doesn't defeat me.
13(12) You uphold me because of my innocence
      you establish me in your presence forever.

14(13) Blessed be ADONAI the God of Isra'el
      from eternity past to eternity future.

      Amen. Amen.

Book II: Psalms 42–72

42 $^{1(0)}$ For the leader. A *maskil* of the descendants of Korach:

2(1) Just as a deer longs for running streams,
      God, I long for you.
3(2) I am thirsty for God, for the living God!
      When can I come and appear before God?

4(3) My tears are my food, day and night,
      while all day people ask me, "Where is your God?"
5(4) I recall, as my feelings well up within me,
      how I'd go with the crowd to the house of God,
      with sounds of joy and praise from the throngs
      observing the festival.

6(5) My soul, why are you so downcast?
      Why are you groaning inside me?
      Hope in God, since I will praise him again
      for the salvation that comes from his presence.

⁷⁽⁶⁾ My God, when I feel so downcast,
I remind myself of you
from the land of Yarden, from the peaks of Hermon,
from the hill Mizar.

⁸⁽⁷⁾ Deep is calling to deep
at the thunder of your waterfalls;
all your surging rapids and waves
are sweeping over me.

⁹⁽⁸⁾ By day ADONAI commands his grace,
and at night his song is with me
as a prayer to the God of my life.

¹⁰⁽⁹⁾ I say to God my Rock,
"Why have you forgotten me?
Why must I go about mourning,
under pressure by the enemy?

¹¹⁽¹⁰⁾ My adversaries' taunts make me feel
as if my bones were crushed,
as they ask me all day long,
'Where is your God?' "

¹²⁽¹¹⁾ My soul, why are you so downcast?
Why are you groaning inside me?
Hope in God, since I will praise him again
for being my Savior and God.

43 ¹ Judge me, God, and plead my cause
against a faithless nation.
Rescue me from those who deceive
and from those who are unjust.

² For you are the God of my strength;
why have you thrust me aside?
Why must I go about mourning,
under pressure by the enemy?

³ Send out your light and your truth;
let them be my guide;
let them lead me to your holy mountain,
to the places where you live.

⁴ Then I will go to the altar of God,
to God, my joy and delight;
I will praise you on the lyre,
God, my God.

⁵ My soul, why are you so downcast?
Why are you groaning inside me?
Hope in God, since I will praise him again
for being my Savior and God.

44 ¹⁽⁰⁾ For the leader. By the descendants of Korach. A *maskil*:

²⁽¹⁾ God, we heard it with our ears;
our fathers told us about it —
a deed which you did in their days,
back in days of old.

³⁽²⁾ With your hand you drove out nations
to plant them in [the land],
you crushed peoples
to make room for them.

⁴⁽³⁾ For not by their own swords
did they conquer the land,
nor did their own arm
give them victory;
rather, it was your right hand,
your arm and the light of your face;
because you favored them.

⁵⁽⁴⁾ God, you are my king;
command complete victory for Ya'akov.

⁶⁽⁵⁾ Through you we pushed away our foes,
through your name we trampled down our assailants.

⁷⁽⁶⁾ For I don't rely on my bow,
nor can my sword give me victory.

⁸⁽⁷⁾ No, you saved us from our adversaries;
you put to shame those who hate us.

⁹⁽⁸⁾ We will boast in our God all day
and give thanks to your name forever.   (*Selah*)

¹⁰⁽⁹⁾ Yet now you have thrust us aside and disgraced us;
you don't march out with our armies.

¹¹⁽¹⁰⁾ You make us retreat from the adversary,
and those who hate us plunder us at will.

¹²⁽¹¹⁾ You have handed us over like sheep to be eaten
and scattered us among the nations.

¹³⁽¹²⁾ You sell your people for a pittance,
you don't even profit on the sale.

¹⁴⁽¹³⁾ You make us an object for our neighbors to mock,
one of scorn and derision to those around us.

¹⁵⁽¹⁴⁾ You make us a byword among the nations;
the peoples jeer at us, shaking their heads.

¹⁶⁽¹⁵⁾ All day long my disgrace is on my mind,
and shame has covered my face

¹⁷⁽¹⁶⁾ at the sound of those who revile and insult,
at the sight of the enemy bent on revenge.

18(17)	Though all this came on us, we did not forget you;
	we have not been false to your covenant;
19(18)	our hearts have not turned back;
	and our steps did not turn away from your path,
20(19)	though you pressed us into a lair of jackals
	and covered us with death-dark gloom.
21(20)	If we had forgotten the name of our God
	or spread out our hands to a foreign god,
22(21)	wouldn't God have discovered this,
	since he knows the secrets of the heart?
23(22)	For your sake we are put to death all day long,
	we are considered sheep to be slaughtered.
24(23)	Wake up, *Adonai*! Why are you asleep?
	Rouse yourself! Don't thrust us off forever.
25(24)	Why are you turning your face away,
	forgetting our pain and misery?
26(25)	For we are lying flat in the dust,
	our bodies cling to the ground.
27(26)	Get up, and come to help us!
	For the sake of your grace, redeem us!

45 ^1(0) For the leader. Set to "Lilies." By the descendants of Korach. A *maskil*. A lovesong:

2(1)	My heart is stirred by a noble theme;
	I address my verses to the king;
	my tongue is the pen of an expert scribe.
3(2)	You are the most handsome of men;
	gracious speech flows from your lips.
	For God has blessed you forever.
4(3)	Warrior, strap your sword at your thigh;
	[gird on] your splendor and majesty.
5(4)	In your majesty, succeed, ride on
	in the cause of truth, meekness and righteousness.
	May your right hand teach you awesome things.
6(5)	Your arrows are sharp. The people fall under you,
	as they penetrate the hearts of the king's enemies.
7(6)	Your throne, God, will last forever and ever;
	you rule your kingdom with a scepter of equity.
8(7)	You have loved righteousness and hated wickedness.
	Therefore God, your God, has anointed you
	with the oil of joy in preference to your companions.
9(8)	Your robes are all fragrant with myrrh, aloes and cassia;
	from ivory palaces stringed instruments bring you joy.

46

10(9)   Daughters of kings are among your favorites;
          at your right stands the queen in gold from Ofir.

11(10)   Listen, daughter! Think, pay attention!
          Forget your own people and your father's house,
12(11)   and the king will desire your beauty;
          for he is your lord, so honor him.
13(12)   Then the daughter of Tzor, the richest of peoples,
          will court your favor with gifts.

14(13)   Inside [the palace], the king's daughter looks splendid,
          attired in checker-work embroidered with gold.
15(14)   In brocade, she will be led to the king,
          to you, with the virgins in her retinue.
16(15)   They will be led in with gladness and joy,
          they will enter the king's palace.
17(16)   You will have sons to succeed your ancestors;
          you will make them princes in all the land.
18(17)   I will make your name known through all generations;
          thus the peoples will praise you forever and ever.

46 ¹⁽⁰⁾ For the leader. By the descendants of Korach. On *'alamot* [high-pitched musical instruments?]. A song:

2(1)   God is our refuge and strength,
          an ever-present help in trouble.
3(2)   Therefore we are unafraid,
          even if the earth gives way,
          even if the mountains tumble
          into the depths of the sea,
4(3)   even if its waters rage and foam,
          and mountains shake at its turbulence.   (*Selah*)

5(4)   There is a river whose streams
          gladden the city of God,
          the holy habitation of *'Elyon* —
6(5)   God is in the city.
          It will not be moved —
          when daybreak comes, God will help it.
7(6)   Nations were in turmoil,
          kingdoms were moved;
          his voice thundered forth,
          and the earth melted away.

8(7)   A*DONAI-Tzva'ot* is with us,
          our fortress, the God of Ya'akov.   (*Selah*)

47

9(8)	Come and see the works of *Adonai*,
	the astounding deeds he has done on the earth.
10(9)	To the ends of the earth he makes wars cease —
	he breaks the bow, snaps the spear,
	burns the shields in the fire.
11(10)	"Desist, and learn that I am God,
	supreme over the nations,
	supreme over the earth."

12(11) *Adonai-Tzva'ot* is with us,
our fortress, the God of Ya'akov.   *(Selah)*

47 $^{1(0)}$ For the leader. A psalm of the descendants of Korach:

2(1)   Clap your hands, all you peoples!
Shout to God with cries of joy!

3(2)   For *Adonai 'Elyon* is awesome,
a great king over all the earth.

4(3)   He makes peoples subject to us,
puts nations under our feet.

5(4)   He chooses our heritage for us,
the pride of Ya'akov, whom he loves.   *(Selah)*

6(5)   God goes up to shouts of acclaim,
Adonai to a blast on the *shofar*.

7(6)   Sing praises to God, sing praises!
Sing praises to our king, sing praises!

8(7)   For God is king of all the earth;
sing praises in a *maskil*.

9(8)   God rules the nations;
God sits on his holy throne.

10(9) The leaders of the people gather together,
the people of the God of Avraham;
for the rulers of the earth belong to God,
who is exalted on high.

48 $^{1(0)}$ A song. A psalm of the descendants of Korach:

2(1)   Great is *Adonai*
and greatly to be praised,
in the city of our God,
his holy mountain,

3(2)   beautiful in its elevation,
the joy of all the earth,
Mount Tziyon, in the far north,
the city of the great king.

4(3) In its citadels God
has been revealed as a strong defense.
5(4) For the kings met by agreement;
together they advanced.
6(5) They saw and were filled with consternation;
terrified, they took to flight.
7(6) Trembling took hold of them,
pains like those of a woman in labor,
8(7) as when the wind out of the east
wrecks the "Tarshish" ships.
9(8) We heard it, and now we see for ourselves
in the city of *Adonai-Tzva'ot*,
in the city of our God.
May God establish it forever. *(Selah)*

10(9) God, within your temple
we meditate on your grace.
11(10) God, your praise, like your name,
extends to the ends of the earth.
Your right hand is filled with righteousness.
12(11) Let Mount Tziyon rejoice,
let the daughters of Y'hudah be glad,
because of your judgment [on the enemy].

13(12) Walk through Tziyon, go all around it;
count how many towers it has.
14(13) Note its ramparts, pass through its citadels,
so that you can tell generations to come
15(14) that such is God, our God forever;
he will guide us eternally.

49 1(0) For the leader. A psalm of the descendants of Korach:

2(1) Hear this, all you peoples!
Listen, everyone living on earth,
3(2) regardless of whether low or high,
regardless of whether rich or poor!
4(3) My mouth is about to speak wisdom;
my heart's deepest thoughts will give understanding.
5(4) I will listen with care to [God's] parable,
I will set my enigma to the music of the lyre.

6(5) Why should I fear when the days bring trouble,
when the evil of my pursuers surrounds me,
7(6) the evil of those who rely on their wealth
and boast how rich they are?

8(7) No one can ever redeem his brother
or give God a ransom for him,
9(8) because the price for him is too high
(leave the idea completely alone!)
10(9) to have him live on eternally
and never see the pit.
11(10) For he can see that wise men will die,
likewise the fool and the brute will perish
and leave their wealth to others.
12(11) They think their homes will last forever,
their dwellings through all generations;
they give their own names to their estates.
13(12) But people, even rich ones, will live only briefly;
then, like animals, they will die.
14(13) This is the manner of life of the foolish
and those who come after, approving their words. *(Selah)*
15(14) Like sheep, they are destined for Sh'ol;
death will be their shepherd.
The upright will rule them in the morning;
and their forms will waste away in Sh'ol,
until they need no dwelling.
16(15) But God will redeem me from Sh'ol's control,
because he will receive me. *(Selah)*

17(16) Don't be afraid when someone gets rich,
when the wealth of his family grows.
18(17) For when he dies, he won't take it with him;
his wealth will not go down after him.
19(18) True, while he lived, he thought himself happy —
people praise you when you do well for yourself —
20(19) but he will join his ancestors' generations
and never again see light.
21(20) People, even rich ones, can fail to grasp
that, like animals, they will die.

50 1(0) A psalm of Asaf:

(1) The Mighty One, God, *Adonai*, is speaking,
summoning the world from east to west.
2 Out of Tziyon, the perfection of beauty,
God is shining forth.
3 Our God is coming and not staying silent.
With a fire devouring ahead of him
and a great storm raging around him,
4 he calls to the heavens above and to earth,
in order to judge his people.

5   "Gather to me my faithful,
    those who made a covenant with me by sacrifice."

6   The heavens proclaim his righteousness,
    for God himself is judge.   (*Selah*)

7   "Listen, my people, I am speaking:
    Isra'el, I am testifying against you,
    I, God, your God.
8   I am not rebuking you for your sacrifices;
    your burnt offerings are always before me.
9   I have no need for a bull from your farm
    or for male goats from your pens;
10 for all forest creatures are mine already,
    as are the animals on a thousand hills;
11 I know all the birds in the mountains;
    whatever moves in the fields is mine.
12 If I were hungry, I would not tell you;
    for the world is mine, and everything in it.
13 Do I eat the flesh of bulls
    or drink the blood of goats?
14 Offer thanksgiving as your sacrifice to God,
    pay your vows to the Most High,
15 and call on me when you are in trouble;
    I will deliver you, and you will honor me."

16 But to the wicked God says:
    "What right do you have to proclaim my laws
    or take my covenant on your lips,
17 when you so hate to receive instruction
    and fling my words behind you?
18 When you see a thief, you join up with him,
    you throw in your lot with adulterers,
19 you give your mouth free rein for evil
    and harness your tongue to deceit;
20 you sit and speak against your kinsman,
    you slander your own mother's son.
21 When you do such things, should I stay silent?
    You may have thought I was just like you;
    but I will rebuke and indict you to your face.
22 Consider this, you who forget God,
    or I will tear you to pieces, with no one to save you.

23 "Whoever offers thanksgiving
    as his sacrifice honors me;
    and to him who goes the right way
    I will show the salvation of God."

51 ¹⁽⁰⁾ For the leader. A psalm of David, ² when Natan the prophet came to him after his affair with Bat-Sheva:

3(1)   God, in your grace, have mercy on me;
       in your great compassion, blot out my crimes.
4(2)   Wash me completely from my guilt,
       and cleanse me from my sin.
5(3)   For I know my crimes,
       my sin confronts me all the time.

6(4)   Against you, you only, have I sinned
       and done what is evil from your perspective;
       so that you are right in accusing me
       and justified in passing sentence.

7(5)   True, I was born guilty,
       was a sinner from the moment my mother conceived me.
8(6)   Still, you want truth in the inner person;
       so make me know wisdom in my inmost heart.

9(7)   Sprinkle me with hyssop, and I will be clean;
       wash me, and I will be whiter than snow.
10(8) Let me hear the sound of joy and gladness,
       so that the bones you crushed can rejoice.
11(9) Turn away your face from my sins,
       and blot out all my crimes.

12(10) Create in me a clean heart, God;
       renew in me a resolute spirit.
13(11) Don't thrust me away from your presence,
       don't take your *Ruach Kodesh* away from me.
14(12) Restore my joy in your salvation,
       and let a willing spirit uphold me.
15(13) Then I will teach the wicked your ways,
       and sinners will return to you.

16(14) Rescue me from the guilt of shedding blood,
       God, God of my salvation!
       Then my tongue will sing
       about your righteousness —
17(15) *Adonai*, open my lips;
       then my mouth will praise you.

18(16) For you don't want sacrifices, or I would give them;
       you don't take pleasure in burnt offerings.
19(17) My sacrifice to God is a broken spirit;
       God, you won't spurn a broken, chastened heart.

²⁰⁽¹⁸⁾ In your good pleasure, make Tziyon prosper;
rebuild the walls of Yerushalayim.
²¹⁽¹⁹⁾ Then you will delight in righteous sacrifices,
in burnt offerings and whole burnt offerings;
then they will offer bulls on your altar.

52 ¹⁽⁰⁾ For the leader. A *maskil* of David, ² when Do'eg from Edom came and told Sha'ul, "David has arrived at the house of Achimelekh":

³⁽¹⁾ Why do you boast of your evil, you tyrant,
when God's mercy is present every day?
⁴⁽²⁾ Your tongue, as sharp as a razor,
plots destruction and works deception.

⁵⁽³⁾ You love evil more than good,
lies rather than speaking uprightly.   (*Selah*)
⁶⁽⁴⁾ You love all words that eat people up,
you deceitful tongue!

⁷⁽⁵⁾ This is why God will strike you down,
seize you, pluck you from your tent
and uproot you from the land of the living.   (*Selah*)

⁸⁽⁶⁾ The righteous will see and be awestruck;
they will jeer at him, saying,
⁹⁽⁷⁾ "This fellow would not make God his refuge,
but trusted in his own great wealth,
relying on his evil plots."

¹⁰⁽⁸⁾ But I am like a leafy olive tree
in the house of God;
I put my trust in the grace of God
forever and ever.

¹¹⁽⁹⁾ I will praise you forever for what you have done,
and I will put my hope in your name;
for this is what is good
in the presence of your faithful.

53 ¹⁽⁰⁾ For the leader. On *machalat*. A *maskil* of David:

²⁽¹⁾ A brutish fool tells himself,
"There isn't any God."
Such people are depraved, all their deeds are vile,
not one of them does what is good.

³⁽²⁾ God looks out from heaven
upon the human race
to see if even one is wise,
if even one seeks God.
⁴⁽³⁾ Every one of them is unclean,
altogether corrupt;
not one of them does what is good,
not a single one.

⁵⁽⁴⁾ Won't these evildoers ever learn?
They devour my people
as if they were eating bread,
and they never call on God!
⁶⁽⁵⁾ They will be gripped with terror,
even though now they are not afraid;
for God will scatter the bones
of him who is besieging you.
You are putting them to shame,
because God has rejected them.

⁷⁽⁶⁾ If only salvation for Isra'el
would come out of Tziyon!
When God restores his people's fortunes,
what joy for Ya'akov! what gladness for Isra'el!

54 ¹⁽⁰⁾ For the leader. With stringed instruments. A *maskil* of David, ² when the Zifim came and told Sha'ul, "David is hiding with us":

³⁽¹⁾ God, deliver me by your name;
in your power, vindicate me.
⁴⁽²⁾ God, hear my prayer;
listen to the words from my mouth.
⁵⁽³⁾ For foreigners are rising against me,
violent men are seeking my life;
they give no thought to God.   (*Selah*)

⁶⁽⁴⁾ But God is helping me;
Adonai is my support.
⁷⁽⁵⁾ May he repay the evil
to those who are lying in wait for me.
In your faithfulness, destroy them!
⁸⁽⁶⁾ Then I will generously sacrifice to you;
I will praise your name, ADONAI,
because it is good,
⁹⁽⁷⁾ because he rescued me from all trouble,
and my eyes look with triumph at my enemies.

55 ¹⁽¹⁾ For the leader. With stringed instruments. A *maskil* of David:

²⁽¹⁾ Listen, God, to my prayer!
    Don't hide yourself from my plea!
³⁽²⁾ Pay attention to me, and answer me!

    I am panic-stricken as I make my complaint,
    I shudder ⁴⁽³⁾ at how the enemy shouts,
    at how the wicked oppress;
    for they keep heaping trouble on me
    and angrily tormenting me.
⁵⁽⁴⁾ My heart within me is pounding in anguish,
    the terrors of death press down on me,
⁶⁽⁵⁾ fear and trembling overwhelm me,
    horror covers me.

⁷⁽⁶⁾ I said, "I wish I had wings like a dove!
    Then I could fly away and be at rest.
⁸⁽⁷⁾ Yes, I would flee to a place far off,
    I would stay in the desert.   (*Selah*)
⁹⁽⁸⁾ I would quickly find me a shelter
    from the raging wind and storm."

¹⁰⁽⁹⁾ Confuse, *Adonai*, confound their speech!
    For I see violence and fighting in the city.
¹¹⁽¹⁰⁾ Day and night they go about its walls;
    within are malice and mischief.
¹²⁽¹¹⁾ Ruin is rife within it,
    oppression and fraud never leave its streets.

¹³⁽¹²⁾ For it was not an enemy who insulted me;
    if it had been, I could have borne it.
    It was not my adversary who treated me with scorn;
    if it had been, I could have hidden myself.
¹⁴⁽¹³⁾ But it was you, a man of my own kind,
    my companion, whom I knew well.

¹⁵⁽¹⁴⁾ We used to share our hearts with each other;
    in the house of God we walked with the crowd.

¹⁶⁽¹⁵⁾ May he put death on them;
    let them go down alive to Sh'ol;
    for evil is in their homes
    and also in their hearts.

¹⁷⁽¹⁶⁾ But I will call on God,
    and *Adonai* will save me.

18(17)	Evening, morning and noon I complain
	and moan; but he hears my voice.
19(18)	He redeems me and gives me peace,
	so that no one can come near me.
	For there were many who fought me.
20(19)	God will hear and will humble them,
	yes, he who has sat on his throne from the start.	*(Selah)*
	For they never change,
	and they don't fear God.

21(20)	[My companion] attacked those
	who were at peace with him;
	he broke his solemn word.
22(21)	What he said sounded smoother than butter,
	but his heart was at war.
	His words seemed more soothing than oil,
	but in fact they were sharp swords.

23(22)	Unload your burden on ADONAI,
	and he will sustain you.
	He will never permit
	the righteous to be moved.

24(23)	But you will bring them down, God,
	into the deepest pit.
	Those men, so bloodthirsty and treacherous,
	will not live out half their days.

| | But for my part, [ADONAI,] |
| | I put my trust in you. |

56 ¹⁽⁰⁾ For the leader. Set to "The Silent Dove in the Distance." By David; a *mikhtam*, when the P'lishtim captured him in Gat:

2(1)	Show me favor, God;
	for people are trampling me down —
	all day they fight and press on me.
3(2)	Those who are lying in wait for me
	would trample on me all day.
	For those fighting against me are many.

	Most High, ⁴⁽³⁾ when I am afraid,
	I put my trust in you.
5(4)	In God — I praise his word —
	in God I trust; I have no fear;
	what can human power do to me?

6(5) All day long they twist my words;
      their only thought is to harm me.
7(6) They gather together and hide themselves,
      spying on my movements, hoping to kill me.
8(7) Because of their crime, they cannot escape;
      in anger, God, strike down the peoples.
9(8) You have kept count of my wanderings;
      store my tears in your water-skin —
      aren't they already recorded in your book?
10(9) Then my enemies will turn back
      on the day when I call;
      this I know: that God is for me.

11(10) In God — I praise his word —
       in ADONAI — I praise his word —
12(11) in God I trust; I have no fear;
       what can mere humans do to me?

13(12) God, I have made vows to you;
       I will fulfill them with thank offerings to you.
14(13) For you rescued me from death,
       you kept my feet from stumbling,
       so that I can walk in God's presence,
       in the light of life.

57 $^{1(0)}$ For the leader. Set to "Do Not Destroy." By David, a *mikhtam*, when he fled from Sha'ul into the cave:

2(1) Show me favor, God, show me favor;
      for in you I have taken refuge.
      Yes, I will find refuge in the shadow of your wings
      until the storms have passed.
3(2) I call to God, the Most High,
      to God, who is accomplishing his purpose for me.

4(3) He will send from heaven and save me
      when those who would trample me down mock me.   (*Selah*)
      God will send his grace and his truth.

5(4) I am surrounded by lions,
      I am lying down among people breathing fire,
      men whose teeth are spears and arrows
      and their tongues sharp-edged swords.

6(5) Be exalted, God, above heaven!
      May your glory be over all the earth!

57

7(6)   They prepared a snare for my feet,
        but I am bending over [to avoid it].
        They dug a pit ahead of me,
        but they fell into it themselves.   *(Selah)*

8(7)   My heart is steadfast, God, steadfast.
        I will sing and make music.
9(8)   Awake, my glory! Awake, lyre and lute!
        I will awaken the dawn.

10(9)   I will thank you, *Adonai*, among the peoples;
        I will make music to you among the nations.
11(10) For your grace is great, all the way to heaven,
        and your truth, all the way to the skies.

12(11) Be exalted, God, above heaven!
        May your glory be over all the earth!

58 ^{1(0)} For the leader. Set to "Do Not Destroy." By David, a *mikhtam*:

2(1)   [Rulers,] does your silence really speak justice?
        Are you judging people fairly?
3(2)   [No!] In your hearts you devise wrongs,
        your hands dispense violence in the land.

4(3)   From the womb, the wicked are estranged,
        liars on the wrong path since birth.
5(4)   Their venom is like snake's venom;
        they are like a serpent that stops its ears,
6(5)   so as not to hear the voice of the charmer,
        no matter how well he plays.

7(6)   God, break their teeth in their mouth!
        Shatter the fangs of these lions, A_DONAI_!
8(7)   May they vanish like water that drains away.
        May their arrows be blunted when they aim their bows.
9(8)   May they be like a slug that melts as it moves,
        like a stillborn baby that never sees the sun.
10(9)   Before your cook-pots feel the heat of the burning thorns,
        may he blow them away, green and blazing alike.

11(10) The righteous will rejoice to see vengeance done,
        they will wash their feet in the blood of the wicked;
12(11) and people will say, "Yes, the righteous are rewarded;
        there is, after all, a God who judges the earth."

59 [1(0)] For the leader. Set to "Do Not Destroy." By David; a *mikhtam*, when Sha'ul sent men to keep watch on David's house in order to kill him:

[2(1)] My God, rescue me from my enemies!
Lift me up, out of reach of my foes!
[3(2)] Rescue me from evildoers,
save me from bloodthirsty men.
[4(3)] For there they are, lying in wait to kill me.
Openly they gather themselves against me,
and not because I committed a crime
or sinned, ADONAI.
[5(4)] For no fault of mine, they run and prepare.
Awaken to help me, and see!
[6(5)] You, ADONAI *Elohei-Tzva'ot*,
God of Isra'el,
arouse yourself to punish all the nations;
spare none of those wicked traitors.   (*Selah*)

[7(6)] They return at nightfall, snarling like dogs
as they go around the city.
[8(7)] Look what pours out of their mouth,
what swords are on their lips,
[as they say to themselves,]
"No one is listening, anyway."
[9(8)] But you, ADONAI, laugh at them,
you mock all the nations.

[10(9)] My Strength, I will watch for you,
for God is my fortress.
[11(10)] God, who gives me grace, will come to me;
God will let me gaze in triumph at my foes.

[12(11)] Don't kill them, or my people will forget;
instead, by your power, make them wander to and fro;
but bring them down, *Adonai* our Shield,
[13(12)] for the sins their mouths make with each word from their lips.
Let them be trapped by their pride
for the curses and falsehoods they utter.
[14(13)] Finish them off in wrath,
finish them off, put an end to them,
and let them know to the ends of the earth
that God is Ruler in Ya'akov.   (*Selah*)

[15(14)] They return at nightfall, snarling like dogs
as they go around the city.
[16(15)] They roam about, looking for food,
prowling all night if they don't get their fill.

¹⁷⁽¹⁶⁾ But as for me, I will sing of your strength;
in the morning I will sing aloud of your grace.
For you are my fortress,
a refuge when I am in trouble.
¹⁸⁽¹⁷⁾ My Strength, I will sing praises to you,
for God is my fortress, God, who gives me grace.

60 ¹⁽⁰⁾ For the leader. Set to "Lily of Testimony." A *mikhtam* of David for teaching about ² when he fought with Aram-Naharayim and with Aram-Tzovah, and Yo'av returned and killed 12,000 from Edom in the Salt Valley:

³⁽¹⁾ God, you rejected us; you crushed us;
you were angry; but now revive us.
⁴⁽²⁾ You made the land shake, split it apart;
now repair the rifts, for it is collapsing.
⁵⁽³⁾ You made your people suffer hard times,
had us drink a wine that made us stagger.

⁶⁽⁴⁾ To those who fear you because of the truth
you gave a banner to rally around,   (*Selah*)
⁷⁽⁵⁾ so that those you love could be rescued;
so save with your right hand, and answer us!

⁸⁽⁶⁾ God in his holiness spoke,
and I took joy [in his promise]:
"I will divide Sh'khem
and determine the shares in the Sukkot Valley.
⁹⁽⁷⁾ Gil'ad is mine and M'nasheh mine,
Efrayim my helmet, Y'hudah my scepter.
¹⁰⁽⁸⁾ Mo'av is my washpot; on Edom I throw my shoe;
P'leshet, be crushed because of me!"

¹¹⁽⁹⁾ Who will bring me into the fortified city?
Who will lead me to Edom?
¹²⁽¹⁰⁾ God, have you rejected us?
You don't go out with our armies, God.
¹³⁽¹¹⁾ Help us against our enemy,
for human help is worthless.
¹⁴⁽¹²⁾ With God's help we will fight valiantly,
for he will trample our enemies.

61 ¹⁽⁰⁾ For the leader. With stringed instruments. By David:

²⁽¹⁾ Hear my cry, God;
listen to my prayer.

³⁽²⁾ From the end of the earth, with fainting heart,
I call out to you.
Set me down on a rock
far above where I am now.

⁴⁽³⁾ For you have been a refuge for me,
a tower of strength in the face of the foe.
⁵⁽⁴⁾ I will live in your tent forever
and find refuge in the shelter of your wings.   (*Selah*)
⁶⁽⁵⁾ For you, God, have heard my vows;
you have given me the heritage of those who fear your name.

⁷⁽⁶⁾ Prolong the life of the king!
May his years go on for many generations.
⁸⁽⁷⁾ May he be enthroned in God's presence forever!
Appoint grace and truth to preserve him!
⁹⁽⁸⁾ Then I will sing praise to your name forever,
as day after day I fulfill my vows.

62 ¹⁽⁰⁾ For the leader. Set in the style of Y'dutun. A psalm of David:

²⁽¹⁾ My soul waits in silence for God alone;
my salvation comes from him.
³⁽²⁾ He alone is my rock and salvation,
my stronghold; I won't be greatly moved.

⁴⁽³⁾ How long will you assail a person
in order to murder him, all of you,
as if he were a sagging wall
or a shaky fence?

⁵⁽⁴⁾ They only want to shake him from his height,
they take delight in lying —
with their mouths they bless,
but inwardly they curse.   (*Selah*)

⁶⁽⁵⁾ My soul, wait in silence for God alone,
because my hope comes from him.
⁷⁽⁶⁾ He alone is my rock and salvation,
my stronghold; I won't be moved.

⁸⁽⁷⁾ My safety and honor rest on God.
My strong rock and refuge are in God.
⁹⁽⁸⁾ Trust in him, people, at all times;
pour out your heart before him;
God is a refuge for us.   (*Selah*)

¹⁰⁽⁹⁾ Ordinary folks are merely a breath
and important people a sham;
if you lay them on a balance-scale, they go up —
both together are lighter than nothing.

¹¹⁽¹⁰⁾ Don't put your trust in extortion,
don't put false hopes in robbery;
even if wealth increases,
don't set your heart on it.

¹²⁽¹¹⁾ God has spoken once, I have heard it twice:
strength belongs to God.

¹³⁽¹²⁾ Also to you, *Adonai*, belongs grace;
for you reward all as their deeds deserve.

63 ¹⁽⁰⁾ A psalm of David, when he was in the desert of Y'hudah:

²⁽¹⁾ O God, you are my God;
I will seek you eagerly.
My heart thirsts for you,
my body longs for you
in a land parched and exhausted,
where no water can be found.

³⁽²⁾ I used to contemplate you in the sanctuary,
seeing your power and glory;

⁴⁽³⁾ for your grace is better than life.
My lips will worship you.

⁵⁽⁴⁾ Yes, I will bless you as long as I live;
in your name I will lift up my hands.

⁶⁽⁵⁾ I am as satisfied as with rich food;
my mouth praises you with joy on my lips

⁷⁽⁶⁾ when I remember you on my bed
and meditate on you in the night watches.

⁸⁽⁷⁾ For you have been my help;
in the shadow of your wings I rejoice;

⁹⁽⁸⁾ my heart clings to you;
your right hand supports me.

¹⁰⁽⁹⁾ But those who seek to destroy my life —
may they go to the lowest parts of the earth.

¹¹⁽¹⁰⁾ May they be given over to the power of the sword;
may they become prey for jackals.

¹²⁽¹¹⁾ But the king will rejoice in God.
Everyone who swears by him will exult,
for the mouths of liars will be silenced.

64 ¹⁽⁰⁾ For the leader. A psalm of David:

²⁽¹⁾ Hear my voice, God, as I plead:
preserve my life from fear of the enemy.
³⁽²⁾ Hide me from the secret intrigues of the wicked
and the open insurrection of evildoers.
⁴⁽³⁾ They sharpen their tongues like a sword;
they aim their arrows, poisoned words,
⁵⁽⁴⁾ in order to shoot from cover at the innocent,
shooting suddenly and fearing nothing.
⁶⁽⁵⁾ They support each other's evil plans;
they talk of hiding snares
and ask, "Who would see them?"
⁷⁽⁶⁾ They search for ways to commit crimes,
bringing their diligent search to completion
when each of them has thought it through
in the depth of his heart.

⁸⁽⁷⁾ Suddenly God shoots them down with an arrow,
leaving them with wounds;
⁹⁽⁸⁾ their own tongues make them stumble.
All who see them shake their heads.
¹⁰⁽⁹⁾ Everyone is awestruck —
they acknowledge that it is God at work,
they understand what he has done.
¹¹⁽¹⁰⁾ The righteous will rejoice in ADONAI;
they will take refuge in him;
all the upright in heart will exult.

65 ¹⁽⁰⁾ For the leader. A psalm of David. A song:

²⁽¹⁾ To you, God, in Tziyon, silence is praise;
and vows to you are to be fulfilled.
³⁽²⁾ You who listen to prayer,
to you all living creatures come.
⁴⁽³⁾ When deeds of wickedness overwhelm me,
you will atone for our crimes.

⁵⁽⁴⁾ How blessed are those you choose and bring near,
so that they can remain in your courtyards!
We will be satisfied with the goodness of your house,
the Holy Place of your temple.
⁶⁽⁵⁾ It is just that you answer us with awesome deeds,
God of our salvation,
you in whom all put their trust,
to the ends of the earth and on distant seas.

⁷⁽⁶⁾ By your strength you set up the mountains.
You are clothed with power.
⁸⁽⁷⁾ You still the roaring of the seas,
their crashing waves, and the peoples' turmoil.
⁹⁽⁸⁾ This is why those living at the ends of the earth
stand in awe of your signs.
The places where the sun rises and sets
you cause to sing for joy.

¹⁰⁽⁹⁾ You care for the earth and water it,
you enrich it greatly;
with the river of God, full of water,
you provide them grain and prepare the ground.
¹¹⁽¹⁰⁾ Soaking its furrows and settling its soil,
you soften it with showers and bless its growth.
¹²⁽¹¹⁾ You crown the year with your goodness,
your tracks overflow with richness.
¹³⁽¹²⁾ The desert pastures drip water,
the hills are wrapped with joy,
¹⁴⁽¹³⁾ the meadows are clothed with flocks
and the valleys blanketed with grain,
so they shout for joy and break into song.

66 ¹⁽⁰⁾ For the leader. A song. A psalm:

⁽¹⁾ Shout to God, all the earth!
² Sing the glory of his name,
make his praise glorious.
³ Tell God, "How awesome are your deeds!
At your great power, your enemies cringe.
⁴ All the earth bows down to you,
sings praises to you, sings praises to your name."   (*Selah*)

⁵ Come and see what God has done,
his awesome dealings with humankind.
⁶ He turned the sea into dry land.
They passed through the river on foot;
there we rejoiced in him.
⁷ With his power he rules forever;
his eyes keep watch on the nations.
Let no rebel arise to challenge him.   (*Selah*)

⁸ Bless our God, you peoples!
Let the sound of his praise be heard!
⁹ He preserves our lives
and keeps our feet from stumbling.

10 For you, God, have tested us,
   refined us as silver is refined.
11 You brought us into the net
   and bound our bodies fast.
12 You made men ride over our heads;
   we went through fire and water.
   But you brought us out
   to a place of plenty.

13 I will come into your house with burnt offerings,
   I will fulfill my vows to you,
14 those my lips pronounced and my mouth spoke
   when I was in distress.
15 I will offer you burnt offerings of fattened animals,
   along with the sweet smoke of rams;
   I will offer bulls and goats.   *(Selah)*

16 Come and listen, all you who fear God,
   and I will tell what he has done for me.
17 I cried out to him with my mouth,
   his praise was on my tongue.
18 Had I cherished evil thoughts,
   Adonai would not have listened.
19 But in fact, God did listen;
   he paid attention to my prayer.
20 Blessed be God, who did not reject my prayer
   or turn his grace away from me.

67 ¹⁽⁰⁾ For the leader. With stringed instruments. A psalm. A song:

2(1) God, be gracious to us, and bless us.
     May he make his face shine toward us,   *(Selah)*
3(2) so that your way may be known on earth,
     your salvation among all nations.

4(3) Let the peoples give thanks to you, God;
     let the peoples give thanks to you, all of them.
5(4) Let the nations be glad and shout for joy,
     for you will judge the peoples fairly
     and guide the nations on earth.   *(Selah)*

6(5) Let the peoples give thanks to you, God;
     let the peoples give thanks to you, all of them.
7(6) The earth has yielded its harvest;
     may God, our God, bless us.
8(7) May God continue to bless us,
     so that all the ends of the earth will fear him.

68 [1(0)] For the leader. A psalm of David. A song:

[2(1)] Let God arise, let his enemies be scattered;
let those who hate him flee from his presence.
[3(2)] Drive them away as smoke is driven away;
like wax melting in the presence of a fire,
let the wicked perish in the presence of God.
[4(3)] But let the righteous rejoice and be glad in God's presence;
yes, let them exult and rejoice.

[5(4)] Sing to God, sing praises to his name;
extol him who rides on the clouds
by his name, *Yah*;
and be glad in his presence.

[6(5)] God, in his holy dwelling,
is a father to orphans and defender of widows.
[7(6)] God gives homes to those who are alone
and leads prisoners out into prosperity.
But rebels must live in a parched wasteland.

[8(7)] God, when you went out at the head of your people,
when you marched out through the wilderness, (*Selah*)
[9(8)] the earth quaked, and rain poured from the sky,
at the presence of God.
Even Sinai [shook] at the presence of God,
the God of Isra'el.
[10(9)] You rained down showers in plenty, God;
when your heritage was weary, you restored it.
[11(10)] Your flock settled in it;
in your goodness, God, you provided for the poor.

[12(11)] *Adonai* gives the command;
the women with the good news are a mighty army.
[13(12)] Kings and their armies are fleeing, fleeing,
while the women at home divide the spoil.
[14(13)] Even if you lie among the animal stalls,
there are wings of a dove covered with silver
and its plumes with yellow gold.
[15(14)] When *Shaddai* scatters kings there,
snow falls on Tzalmon.

[16(15)] You mighty mountain, Mount Bashan!
You rugged mountain, Mount Bashan!
[17(16)] You rugged mountain, why look with envy
at the mountain God wants for his place to live?
Truly, *Adonai* will live there forever.

18(17) God's chariots are myriads, repeated thousands;
        Adonai is among them as in Sinai, in holiness.
19(18) After you went up into the heights,
        you led captivity captive,
        you took gifts among mankind,
        yes, even among the rebels,
        so that *Yah*, God, might live there.

20(19) Blessed be *Adonai*!
        Every day he bears our burden,
        does God, our salvation.   (*Selah*)
21(20) Our God is a God who saves;
        from A<small>DONAI</small> *Adonai* comes escape from death.
22(21) God will surely crush the heads of his enemies,
        the hairy crowns of those who continue in their guilt.
23(22) *Adonai* said, "I will bring them back from Bashan,
        I will fetch [those rebels] even from the depths of the sea;
24(23) so that you can wash your feet in their blood,
        and your dogs' tongues too can get their share from your foes.

25(24) They see your processions, God,
        the processions of my God, my king, in holiness.
26(25) The singers are in front, the musicians last,
        in the middle are girls playing tambourines.
27(26) "In choruses, bless God, *Adonai*,
        you whose source is Isra'el."
28(27) There is Binyamin, the youngest, at the head;
        the princes of Y'hudah, crowding along;
        the princes of Z'vulun; the princes of Naftali.

29(28) God, summon your strength!
        Use your strength, God, as you did for us before,
30(29) from your temple in Yerushalayim,
        where kings will bring tribute to you.
31(30) Rebuke the wild beast of the reeds,
        that herd of bulls with their calves, the peoples,
        who ingratiate themselves with bars of silver;
        let him scatter the peoples who take pleasure in fighting.
32(31) Let envoys come from Egypt,
        Let Ethiopia stretch out its hands to God.

33(32) Sing to God, kingdoms of the earth!
        Sing praises to *Adonai*,   (*Selah*)
34(33) to him who rides on the most ancient heavens.
        Listen, as he utters his voice, a mighty voice!
35(34) Acknowledge that strength belongs to God,
        with his majesty over Isra'el and his strength in the skies.

36(35)　　How awe-inspiring you are, God,
　　　　　from your holy places,
　　　　　the God of Isra'el, who gives strength
　　　　　and power to the people.
　　　　　Blessed be God!

69 ¹⁽⁰⁾ For the leader. Set to "Lilies." By David:

2(1)　　Save me, God!
　　　　For the water threatens my life.
3(2)　　I am sinking down in the mud,
　　　　and there is no foothold;
　　　　I have come into deep water;
　　　　the flood is sweeping over me.
4(3)　　I am exhausted from crying,
　　　　my throat is dry and sore,
　　　　my eyes are worn out
　　　　with looking for my God.

5(4)　　Those who hate me for no reason
　　　　outnumber the hairs on my head.
　　　　My persecutors are powerful,
　　　　my enemies accuse me falsely.
　　　　Am I expected to return
　　　　things I didn't steal?

6(5)　　God, you know how foolish I am;
　　　　my guilt is not hidden from you.
7(6)　　Let those who put their hope in you,
　　　　Adonai ELOHIM-Tzva'ot,
　　　　not be put to shame through me;
　　　　let those who are seeking you,
　　　　God of Isra'el,
　　　　not be disgraced through me.

8(7)　　For your sake I suffer insults,
　　　　shame covers my face.
9(8)　　I am estranged from my brothers,
　　　　an alien to my mother's children,
10(9)　　because zeal for your house is eating me up,
　　　　and on me are falling the insults
　　　　of those insulting you.
11(10)　　I weep bitterly, and I fast,
　　　　but that too occasions insults.
12(11)　　I clothe myself with sackcloth
　　　　and become an object of scorn,

13(12) the gossip of those sitting by the town gate,
        the theme of drunkards' songs.

14(13) As for me, ADONAI, let my prayer to you
        come at an acceptable time;
        In your great grace, God, answer me
        with the truth of your salvation.
15(14) Rescue me from the mud!
        Don't let me sink!
        Let me be rescued from those who hate me
        and from the deep water.
16(15) Don't let the floodwaters overwhelm me,
        don't let the deep swallow me up,
        don't let the pit close its mouth over me.

17(16) Answer me, ADONAI, for your grace is good;
        in your great mercy, turn to me.
18(17) Don't hide your face from your servant,
        for I am in trouble; answer me quickly.
19(18) Come near to me, and redeem me;
        ransom me because of my enemies.

20(19) You know how I am insulted,
        shamed and disgraced;
        before you stand all my foes.
21(20) Insults have broken my heart
        to the point that I could die.
        I hoped that someone would show compassion,
        but nobody did;
        and that there would be comforters,
        but I found none.
22(21) They put poison in my food;
        in my thirst, they gave me vinegar to drink.
23(22) Let their dining table
        before them become a snare;
        when they are at peace,
        let it become a trap;
24(23) let their eyes be darkened,
        so that they can't see,
        and let their bodies
        always be stumbling.
25(24) Pour out your fury on them,
        let your fierce anger overtake them.
26(25) Let the place where they live be desolate,
        with no one to live in their tents,
27(26) for persecuting someone you had already stricken,
        for adding to the pain of those you wounded.

28(27) Add guilt to their guilt,
        don't let them enter your righteousness.
29(28) Erase them from the book of life,
        let them not be written with the righteous.

30(29) Meanwhile, I am afflicted and hurting;
        God, let your saving power raise me up.
31(30) I will praise God's name with a song
        and extol him with thanksgiving.

32(31) This will please ADONAI more than a bull,
        with its horns and hoofs.
33(32) The afflicted will see it and rejoice;
        you seeking after God, let your heart revive.
34(33) For ADONAI pays attention to the needy
        and doesn't scorn his captive people.

35(34) Let heaven and earth praise him,
        the seas and whatever moves in them.
36(35) For God will save Tziyon,
        he will build the cities of Y'hudah.
        [His people] will settle there and possess it.
37(36) The descendants of his servants will inherit it,
        and those who love his name will live there.

70 ¹⁽⁰⁾ For the leader. By David. As a reminder:

2(1)   God, rescue me!
        ADONAI, hurry and help me!

3(2)   May those who seek my life
        be disgraced and humiliated.
        May those who take pleasure in doing me harm
        be turned back and put to confusion.
4(3)   May those who jeer, "Aha! Aha!"
        withdraw because of their shame.

5(4)   But may all those who seek you
        be glad and take joy in you.
        May those who love your salvation say always,
        "God is great and glorious!"

6(5)   But I am poor and needy;
        God, hurry for me.
        You are my helper and rescuer;
        ADONAI, don't delay!

71 [1] In you, *ADONAI*, I have taken refuge;
let me never be put to shame.
[2] In your righteousness, rescue me;
and help me to escape.
Turn your ear toward me,
and deliver me.

[3] Be for me a sheltering rock,
where I can always come.
You have determined to save me,
because you are my bedrock and stronghold.

[4] My God, help me escape from the power of the wicked,
from the grasp of the unjust and ruthless.
[5] For you are my hope, *Adonai ELOHIM*,
in whom I have trusted since I was young.
[6] From birth I have relied on you;
it was you who took me from my mother's womb.

[7] To many, I am an amazing example;
but you are strong protection for me.
[8] My mouth is full of praise for you,
filled with your glory all day long.

[9] Don't reject me when I grow old;
when my strength fails, don't abandon me.
[10] For my enemies are talking about me,
those seeking my life are plotting together.
[11] They say, "God has abandoned him;
go after him, and seize him,
because no one will save him."
[12] God, don't distance yourself from me!
My God, hurry to help me!
[13] May those who are opposed to me
be put to shame and ruin;
may those who seek to harm me
be covered with scorn and disgrace.

[14] But I, I will always hope
and keep adding to your praise.
[15] All day long my mouth will tell
of your righteous deeds and acts of salvation,
though their number is past my knowing.
[16] I will come in the power of *Adonai ELOHIM*
and recall your righteousness, yours alone.
[17] God, you have taught me since I was young,
and I still proclaim your wonderful works.

18   So now that I'm old, and my hair is gray,
      don't abandon me, God, till I have proclaimed
      your strength to the next generation,
      your power to all who will come,
19   your righteousness too, God,
      which reaches to the heights.
      God, you have done great things;
      who is there like you?
20   You have made me see much trouble and hardship,
      but you will revive me again
      and bring me up from the depths of the earth.
21   You will increase my honor;
      turn and comfort me.

22   As for me, I will praise you with a lyre
      for your faithfulness, my God.
      I will sing praises to you with a lute,
      Holy One of Isra'el.
23   My lips will shout for joy;
      I will sing your praise, because you have redeemed me.
24   All day long my tongue
      will speak of your righteousness.
      For those who are seeking to harm me
      will be put to shame and disgraced.

72 ¹⁽⁰⁾ By Shlomo:

(1)   God, give the king your fairness in judgment,
      endow this son of kings with your righteousness,
2   so that he can govern your people rightly
      and your poor with justice.
3   May mountains and hills provide your people
      with peace through righteousness.
4   May he defend the oppressed among the people,
      save the needy and crush the oppressor.

5   May they fear you as long as the sun endures
      and as long as the moon, through all generations.
6   May he be like rain falling on mown grass,
      like showers watering the land.
7   In his days, let the righteous flourish
      and peace abound, till the moon is no more.
8   May his empire stretch from sea to sea,
      from the [Euphrates] River to the ends of the earth.
9   May desert-dwellers bow before him;
      may his enemies lick the dust.

10 The kings of Tarshish and the coasts will pay him tribute;
    the kings of Sh'va and S'va will offer gifts.
11 Yes, all kings will prostrate themselves before him;
    all nations will serve him.

12 For he will rescue the needy when they cry,
    the poor too and those with none to help them.
13 He will have pity on the poor and needy;
    and the lives of the needy he will save.
14 He will redeem them from oppression and violence;
    their blood will be precious in his view.

15 May [the king] live long!
    May they give him gold from the land of Sh'va!
    May they pray for him continually;
    yes, bless him all day long.
16 May there be an abundance of grain in the land,
    all the way to the tops of the mountains.
    May its crops rustle like the L'vanon.
    May people blossom in the city like the grasses in the fields.
17 May his name endure forever,
    his name, Yinnon, as long as the sun.*
    May people bless themselves in him,
    may all nations call him happy.

18 Blessed be *Adonai*, God,
    the God of Isra'el,
    who alone works wonders.
19 Blessed be his glorious name forever,
    and may the whole earth be filled with his glory.
    Amen. Amen.

20 This completes the prayers of David the son of Yishai.

Book III: Psalms 73–89

73 $^{1(0)}$ A psalm of Asaf:

(1) How good God is to Isra'el,
     to those who are pure in heart!
2   But as for me, I lost my balance,
     my feet nearly slipped,

---
* Or: "May his name flourish/propagate as long as the sun." Jewish tradition considers Yinnon a name of the Messiah.

3   when I grew envious of the arrogant
and saw how the wicked prosper.

4   For when their death comes, it is painless;
and meanwhile, their bodies are healthy;

5   they don't have ordinary people's troubles,
they aren't plagued like others.

6   So for them, pride is a necklace;
and violence clothes them like a robe.

7   Their eyes peep out through folds of fat;
evil thoughts overflow from their hearts.

8   They scoff and speak with malice,
they loftily utter threats.

9   They set their mouths against heaven;
their tongues swagger through the earth.

10   Therefore his people return here
and [thoughtlessly] suck up that whole cup of water.

11   Then they ask, "How does God know?
Does the Most High really have knowledge?"

12   Yes, this is what the wicked are like;
those free of misfortune keep increasing their wealth.

13   It's all for nothing that I've kept my heart clean
and washed my hands, staying free of guilt;

14   for all day long I am plagued;
my punishment comes every morning.

15   If I had said, "I will talk like them,"
I would have betrayed a generation of your children.

16   When I tried to understand all this,
I found it too hard for me —

17   until I went into the sanctuaries of God
and grasped what their destiny would be.

18   Indeed, you place them on a slippery slope
and make them fall to their ruin.

19   How suddenly they are destroyed,
swept away by terrors!

20   They are like a dream when one awakens;
Adonai, when you rouse yourself,
you will despise their phantoms.

21   When I had a sour attitude
and felt stung by pained emotions,

22   I was too stupid to understand;
I was like a brute beast with you.

23 Nevertheless, I am always with you;
    you hold my right hand.
24 You will guide me with your advice;
    and afterwards, you will receive me with honor.

25 Whom do I have in heaven but you?
    And with you, I lack nothing on earth.
26 My mind and body may fail; but God
    is the rock for my mind and my portion forever.

27 Those who are far from you will perish;
    you destroy all who adulterously leave you.
28 But for me, the nearness of God is my good;
    I have made *Adonai ELOHIM* my refuge,
    so that I can tell of all your works.

74 ¹⁽⁰⁾ A *maskil* of Asaf:

⁽¹⁾ Why have you rejected us forever, God,
     with your anger smoking against the sheep you once pastured?
2   Remember your community, which you acquired long ago,
     the tribe you redeemed to be your very own.
     Remember Mount Tziyon, where you came to live.
3   Hurry your steps to these endless ruins,
     to the sanctuary devastated by the enemy.

4   The roar of your foes filled your meeting-place;
     they raised their own banners as a sign of their conquest.
5   The place seemed like a thicket of trees
     when lumbermen hack away with their axes.
6   With hatchet and hammer they banged away,
     smashing all the carved woodwork.
7   They set your sanctuary on fire,
     tore down and profaned the abode of your name.
8   They said to themselves, "We will oppress them completely."
     They have burned down all God's meeting-places in the land.

9   We see no signs, there is no prophet any more;
     none of us knows how long it will last.
10   How much longer, God, will the foe jeer at us?
     Will the enemy insult your name forever?
11   Why do you hold back your hand?
     Draw your right hand from your coat, and finish them off!

12   God has been my king from earliest times,
     acting to save throughout all the earth.

13   By your strength you split the sea in two,
      in the water you smashed sea monsters' heads,
14   you crushed the heads of Livyatan
      and gave it as food to the creatures of the desert.
15   You cut channels for springs and streams,
      you dried up rivers that had never failed.
16   The day is yours, and the night is yours;
      it was you who established light and sun.
17   It was you who fixed all the limits of the earth,
      you made summer and winter.

18   Remember how the enemy scoffs at ADONAI,
      how a brutish people insults your name.
19   Don't hand over the soul of your dove to wild beasts,
      don't forget forever the life of your poor.

20   Look to the covenant, for the land's dark places
      are full of the haunts of violence.
21   Don't let the oppressed retreat in confusion;
      let the poor and needy praise your name.

22   Arise, God, and defend your cause;
      remember how brutish men insult you all day.
23   Don't forget what your foes are saying,
      the ever-rising uproar of your adversaries.

75 [1(0)] For the leader. Set to "Do Not Destroy!" A psalm of Asaf. A song:

2(1)   We give thanks to you, God, we give thanks;
        your name is near, people tell of your wonders.

3(2)   "At the time of my own choice,
        I will dispense justice fairly.
4(3)   When the earth quakes, with all living on it,
        it is I who hold its support-pillars firm."   *(Selah)*

5(4)   To the boastful I say, "Do not boast!"
        and to the wicked, "Don't flaunt your strength!
6(5)   Don't flaunt your strength so proudly;
        don't speak arrogantly, with your nose in the air!
7(6)   For you will not be raised to power
        by those in the east, the west or the desert;
8(7)   since God is the judge; and it is he
        who puts down one and lifts up another.
9(8)   In ADONAI's hand there is a cup of wine,
        foaming, richly spiced;

when he pours it out, all the wicked of the earth
will drain it, drinking it to the dregs."

10(9) But I will always speak out,
singing praises to the God of Ya'akov.

11(10) I will break down the strength of the wicked,
but the strength of the righteous will be raised up.

76 ¹⁽⁰⁾ For the leader. With string music. A psalm of Asaf. A song:

2(1) In Y'hudah God is known;
his name is great in Isra'el.

3(2) His tent is in Shalem,
his place is in Tziyon.

4(3) There he broke the flashing arrows,
the shield, the sword, and the weapons of war.   (*Selah*)

5(4) You are glorious, majestic,
more so than mountains of prey.

6(5) The bravest have been stripped of their spoil
and now are sleeping their final sleep;
not one of these courageous men
finds strength to raise his hands.

7(6) At your rebuke, God of Ya'akov,
riders and horses lie stunned.

8(7) You are fearsome! When once you are angry,
who can stand in your presence?

9(8) You pronounce sentence from heaven;
the earth grows silent with fear

10(9) when God arises to judge,
to save all the humble of the earth.   (*Selah*)

11(10) Human wrath serves only to praise you;
what remains of this wrath you wear as an ornament.

12(11) Make vows to ADONAI your God, and keep them;
all who are around him must bring presents to the one who should be feared.

13(12) He curbs the spirit of princes;
he is fearsome to the kings of the earth.

77 ¹⁽⁰⁾ For the leader. For Y'dutun. A psalm of Asaf:

2(1) I cry aloud to God,
aloud to God; and he hears me.

3(2) On the day of my distress I am seeking *Adonai*;
my hands are lifted up;

my tears flow all night without ceasing;
my heart refuses comfort.

4(3)   When remembering God, I moan;
when I ponder, my spirit fails.   *(Selah)*

5(4)   You hold my eyelids [and keep me from sleeping];
I am too troubled to speak.

6(5)   I think about the days of old,
the years of long ago;

7(6)   in the night I remember my song,
I commune with myself, my spirit inquires:

8(7)   "Will *Adonai* reject forever?
will he never show his favor again?

9(8)   Has his grace permanently disappeared?
Is his word to all generations done away?

10(9)   Has God forgotten to be compassionate?
Has he in anger withheld his mercy?"   *(Selah)*

11(10)   Then I add, "That's my weakness —
[supposing] the Most High's right hand could change."

12(11)   So I will remind myself of *Yah*'s doings;
yes, I will remember your wonders of old.

13(12)   I will meditate on your work
and think about what you have done.

14(13)   God, your way is in holiness.
What god is as great as God?

15(14)   You are the God who does wonders,
you revealed your strength to the peoples.

16(15)   With your arm you redeemed your people,
the descendants of Ya'akov and Yosef.   *(Selah)*

17(16)   The water saw you, God;
the water saw you and writhed in anguish,
agitated to its depths.

18(17)   The clouds poured water, the skies thundered,
and your arrows flashed here and there.

19(18)   The sound of your thunder was in the whirlwind,
the lightning flashes lit up the world,
the earth trembled and shook.

20(19)   Your way went through the sea,
your path through the turbulent waters;
but your footsteps could not be traced.

21(20)   You led your people like a flock
under the care of Moshe and Aharon.

78 [1(0)] A *maskil* of Asaf:

(1)   Listen, my people, to my teaching;
       turn your ears to the words from my mouth.
2   I will speak to you in parables
       and explain mysteries from days of old.

3   The things which we have heard and known,
       and which our fathers told us
4   we will not hide from their descendants;
       we will tell the generation to come
       the praises of A*DONAI* and his strength,
       the wonders that he has performed.

5   He raised up a testimony in Ya'akov
       and established a *Torah* in Isra'el.
       He commanded our ancestors
       to make this known to their children,
6   so that the next generation would know it,
       the children not yet born,
       who would themselves arise
       and tell their own children,
7   who could then put their confidence in God,
       not forgetting God's deeds,
       but obeying his *mitzvot*.
8   Then they would not be like their ancestors,
       a stubborn, rebellious generation,
       a generation with unprepared hearts,
       with spirits unfaithful to God.

9   The people of Efrayim, though armed with bows and arrows,
       turned their backs on the day of battle.
10   They did not keep the covenant of God
       and refused to live by his *Torah*.
11   They forgot what he had done,
       his wonders which he had shown them.

12   He had done wonderful things
       in the presence of their ancestors
       in the land of Egypt,
       in the region of Tzo'an.
13   He split the sea and made them pass through,
       he made the waters stand up like a wall.
14   He also led them by day with a cloud
       and all night long with light from a fire.
15   He broke apart the rocks in the desert
       and let them drink as if from boundless depths;

16   yes, he brought streams out of the rock,
        making the water flow down like rivers.

17   Yet they sinned still more against him,
        rebelling in the wilderness against the Most High;
18   in their hearts they tested God
        by demanding food that would satisfy their cravings.
19   Yes, they spoke against God by asking,
        "Can God spread a table in the desert?
20   True, he struck the rock, and water gushed out,
        until the *vadis* overflowed;
        but what about bread? Can he give that?
        Can he provide meat for his people?"

21   Therefore, when ADONAI heard, he was angry;
        fire blazed up against Ya'akov;
        his anger mounted against Isra'el;
22   because they had no faith in God,
        no trust in his power to save.

23   So he commanded the skies above
        and opened the doors of heaven.
24   He rained down *man* on them as food;
        he gave them grain from heaven —
25   mortals ate the bread of angels;
        he provided for them to the full.

26   He stirred up the east wind in heaven,
        brought on the south wind by his power,
27   and rained down meat on them like dust,
        birds flying thick as the sand on the seashore.
28   He let them fall in the middle of their camp,
        all around their tents.
29   So they ate till they were satisfied;
        he gave them what they craved.
30   They were still fulfilling their craving,
        the food was still in their mouths,
31   when the anger of God rose up against them
        and slaughtered their strongest men,
        laying low the young men of Isra'el.

32   Still, they kept on sinning
        and put no faith in his wonders.
33   Therefore, he ended their days in futility
        and their years in terror.
34   When he brought death among them, they would seek him;
        they would repent and seek God eagerly,

35   remembering that God was their Rock,
    El 'Elyon their Redeemer.

36   But they tried to deceive him with their words,
    they lied to him with their tongues;
37   for their hearts were not right with him,
    and they were unfaithful to his covenant.
38   Yet he, because he is full of compassion,
    forgave their sin and did not destroy;
    many times he turned away his anger
    and didn't rouse all his wrath.
39   So he remembered that they were but flesh,
    a wind that blows past and does not return.

40   How often they rebelled against him in the desert
    and grieved him in the wastelands!
41   Repeatedly they challenged God
    and pained the Holy One of Isra'el.
42   They didn't remember how he used his hand
    on the day he redeemed them from their enemy,
43   how he displayed his signs in Egypt,
    his wonders in the region of Tzo'an.

44   He turned their rivers into blood,
    so they couldn't drink from their streams.
45   He sent swarms of flies, which devoured them,
    and frogs, which destroyed them.
46   He gave their harvest to shearer-worms,
    the fruit of their labor to locusts.
47   He destroyed their vineyards with hail
    and their sycamore-figs with frost.
48   Their cattle too he gave over to the hail
    and their flocks to lightning bolts.

49   He sent over them his fierce anger,
    fury, indignation and trouble,
    with a company of destroying angels
50   to clear a path for his wrath.
    He did not spare them from death,
    but gave them over to the plague,
51   striking all the firstborn in Egypt,
    the firstfruits of their strength in the tents of Ham.

52   But his own people he led out like sheep,
    guiding them like a flock in the desert.
53   He led them safely, and they weren't afraid,
    even when the sea overwhelmed their foes.

54 He brought them to his holy land,
   to the hill-country won by his right hand.
55 He expelled nations before them,
   apportioned them property to inherit
   and made Isra'el's tribes live in their tents.

56 Yet they tested *El 'Elyon*
   and rebelled against him,
   refusing to obey his instructions.
57 They turned away and were faithless, like their fathers;
   they were unreliable, like a bow without tension.
58 They provoked him with their high places
   and made him jealous with their idols.

59 God heard, and he was angry;
   he came to detest Isra'el completely.
60 He abandoned the tabernacle at Shiloh,
   the tent he had made where he could live among people.
61 He gave his strength into exile,
   his pride to the power of the foe.
62 He gave his people over to the sword
   and grew angry with his own heritage.
63 Fire consumed their young men,
   their virgins had no wedding-song,
64 their *cohanim* fell by the sword,
   and their widows could not weep.

65 Then *Adonai* awoke, as if from sleep,
   like a warrior shouting for joy from wine.
66 He struck his foes, driving them back
   and putting them to perpetual shame.

67 Rejecting the tents of Yosef
   and passing over the tribe of Efrayim,
68 he chose the tribe of Y'hudah,
   Mount Tziyon, which he loved.
69 He built his sanctuary like the heights;
   like the earth, he made it to last forever.

70 He chose David to be his servant,
   taking him from the sheep-yards;
71 from tending nursing ewes he brought him
   to shepherd Ya'akov his people,
   Isra'el his heritage.
72 With upright heart he shepherded them
   and guided them with skillful hands.

79 [1(0)] A psalm of Asaf:

[1] God, the pagans have entered your heritage.
They have defiled your holy temple
and turned Yerushalayim into rubble.

[2] They have given the corpses of your servants
as food for the birds in the air,
yes, the flesh of those faithful to you
for the wild animals of the earth.

[3] All around Yerushalayim
they have shed their blood like water,
and no one is left to bury them.

[4] We suffer the taunts of our neighbors,
we are mocked and scorned by those around us.

[5] How long, ADONAI?
Will you be angry forever?
How long will your jealousy burn like fire?

[6] Pour out your wrath on the nations that don't know you,
on the kingdoms that don't call out your name;

[7] for they have devoured Ya'akov
and left his home a waste.

[8] Don't count past iniquities against us,
but let your compassion come quickly to meet us,
for we have been brought very low.

[9] Help us, God of our salvation,
for the sake of the glory of your name.
Deliver us, forgive our sins,
for your name's sake.

[10] Why should the nations ask,
"Where is their God?"

Let the vengeance taken on your servants' shed blood
be known among the nations before our eyes.

[11] Let the groaning of the captives come before you;
by your great strength save those condemned to death.

[12] Repay our neighbors sevenfold where they can feel it
for the insults they inflicted on you, *Adonai*.

[13] Then we, your people and the flock in your pasture,
will give you thanks forever.
From generation to generation
we will proclaim your praise.

80 ^{1(0)} For the leader. Set to "Lilies." A testimony. A psalm of Asaf:

^{2(1)}   Shepherd of Isra'el, listen!
        You who lead Yosef like a flock,
        you whose throne is on the *k'ruvim*,
        shine out!
^{3(2)}   Before Efrayim, Binyamin and M'nasheh,
        rouse your power; and come to save us.
^{4(3)}   God, restore us!
        Make your face shine, and we will be saved.

^{5(4)}   *Adonai*, God of armies, how long
        will you be angry with your people's prayers?
^{6(5)}   You have fed them tears as their bread
        and made them drink tears in abundance.
^{7(6)}   You make our neighbors fight over us,
        and our enemies mock us.
^{8(7)}   God of armies, restore us!
        Make your face shine, and we will be saved.

^{9(8)}   You brought a vine out of Egypt,
        you expelled the nations and planted it,
^{10(9)}   you cleared a space for it;
        then it took root firmly and filled the land.
^{11(10)}   The mountains were covered with its shade,
        the mighty cedars with its branches —
^{12(11)}   it put out branches as far as the sea
        and shoots to the [Euphrates] River.

^{13(12)}   Why did you break down [the vineyard's] wall,
        so that all passing by can pluck [its fruit]?
^{14(13)}   The boar from the forest tears it apart;
        wild creatures from the fields feed on it.

^{15(14)}   God of armies, please come back!
        Look from heaven, see, and tend this vine!
^{16(15)}   Protect what your right hand planted,
        the son you made strong for yourself.
^{17(16)}   It is burned by fire, it is cut down;
        they perish at your frown of rebuke.
^{18(17)}   Help the man at your right hand,
        the son of man you made strong for yourself.

^{19(18)}   Then we won't turn away from you —
        if you revive us, we will call on your name.
^{20(19)}   *Adonai*, God of armies, restore us!
        Make your face shine, and we will be saved.

81 ¹⁽⁰⁾ For the Leader. On the *gittit*. By Asaf:

²⁽¹⁾   Sing for joy to God our strength!
         Shout to the God of Ya'akov!
³⁽²⁾   Start the music! Beat the drum!
         Play the sweet lyre and the lute!
⁴⁽³⁾   Sound the *shofar* at *Rosh-Hodesh*
         and at full moon for the pilgrim feast,
⁵⁽⁴⁾   because this is a law for Isra'el,
         a ruling of the God of Ya'akov.
⁶⁽⁵⁾   He placed it as a testimony in Y'hosef
         when he went out against the land of Egypt.

         I heard an unfamiliar voice say,
⁷⁽⁶⁾   "I lifted the load from his shoulder;
         his hands were freed from the [laborer's] basket.
⁸⁽⁷⁾   You called out when you were in trouble,
         and I rescued you;
         I answered you from the thundercloud;
         I tested you at the M'rivah Spring [by saying,]   *(Selah)*

⁹⁽⁸⁾   "'Hear, my people, while I give you warning!
         Isra'el, if you would only listen to me!
¹⁰⁽⁹⁾   There is not to be with you any foreign god;
         you are not to worship an alien god.
¹¹⁽¹⁰⁾   I am A*DONAI* your God,
         who brought you up from the land of Egypt.
         Open your mouth, and I will fill it.'

¹²⁽¹¹⁾   "But my people did not listen to my voice;
         Isra'el would have none of me.
¹³⁽¹²⁾   So I gave them over to their stubborn hearts,
         to live by their own plans.
¹⁴⁽¹³⁾   How I wish my people would listen to me,
         that Isra'el would live by my ways!
¹⁵⁽¹⁴⁾   I would quickly subdue their enemies
         and turn my hand against their foes.
¹⁶⁽¹⁵⁾   Those who hate A*DONAI* would cringe before him,
         while [Isra'el's] time would last forever.
¹⁷⁽¹⁶⁾   They would be fed with the finest wheat,
         and I would satisfy you with honey from the rocks."

82 ¹⁽⁰⁾ A psalm of Asaf:

⁽¹⁾   *Elohim* [God] stands in the divine assembly;
         there with the *elohim* [judges], he judges:

2   "How long will you go on judging unfairly,
         favoring the wicked?   *(Selah)*

3   Give justice to the weak and fatherless!
         Uphold the rights of the wretched and poor!

4   Rescue the destitute and needy;
         deliver them from the power of the wicked!"

5   They don't know, they don't understand,
         they wander about in darkness;
         meanwhile, all the foundations of the earth
         are being undermined.

6   "My decree is: 'You are *elohim* [gods, judges],
         sons of the Most High all of you.

7   Nevertheless, you will die like mortals;
         like any prince, you will fall.'"

8   Rise up, *Elohim*, and judge the earth;
         for all the nations are yours.

83 ¹⁽⁰⁾ A song. A psalm of Asaf:

2(1)   God, don't remain silent!
         Don't stay quiet, God, or still;

3(2)   because here are your enemies, causing an uproar;
         those who hate you are raising their heads,

4(3)   craftily conspiring against your people,
         consulting together against those you treasure.

5(4)   They say, "Come, let's wipe them out as a nation;
         let the name of Isra'el be remembered no more!"

6(5)   With one mind they plot their schemes;
         the covenant they have made is against you —

7(6)   the tents of Edom and the Yishma'elim,
         Mo'av and the Hagrim,

8(7)   G'val, 'Amon and 'Amalek,
         P'leshet with those living in Tzor;   *(Selah)*

9(8)   Ashur too is allied with them,
         to reinforce the descendants of Lot.

10(9)   Do to them as you did to Midyan,
         to Sisra and Yavin at *Vadi* Kishon —

11(10)   they were destroyed at 'Ein-Dor
         and became manure for the ground.

12(11)   Make their leaders like 'Orev and Ze'ev,
         all their princes like Zevach and Tzalmuna,

13(12) who said, "Let's take possession
of God's meadows for ourselves."

14(13) My God, make them like whirling dust,
like chaff driven by the wind.

15(14) Like fire burning up the forest,
like a flame that sets the mountains ablaze,

16(15) drive them away with your storm,
terrify them with your tempest.

17(16) Fill their faces with shame,
so that they will seek your name, ADONAI.

18(17) Let them be ashamed and fearful forever;
yes, let them perish in disgrace.

19(18) Let them know that you alone,
whose name is ADONAI,
are the Most High over all the earth.

84 1(0) For the leader. On the *gittit*. A psalm of the sons of Korach:

2(1) How deeply loved are your dwelling-places,
ADONAI-*Tzva'ot*!

3(2) My soul yearns, yes, faints with longing
for the courtyards of ADONAI;
my heart and body cry for joy
to the living God.

4(3) As the sparrow finds herself a home
and the swallow her nest, where she lays her young,
[so my resting-place is] by your altars,
ADONAI-*Tzva'ot*, my king and my God.

5(4) How happy are those who live in your house;
they never cease to praise you!   (*Selah*)

6(5) How happy the man whose strength is in you,
in whose heart are [pilgrim] highways.

7(6) Passing through the [dry] Baka Valley,
they make it a place of springs,
and the early rain clothes it with blessings.

8(7) They go from strength to strength
and appear before God in Tziyon.

9(8) ADONAI, God of armies, hear my prayer;
listen, God of Ya'akov.   (*Selah*)

10(9) God, see our shield [the king];
look at the face of your anointed.

11(10)
Better a day in your courtyards
than a thousand [days elsewhere].
Better just standing at the door of my God's house
than living in the tents of the wicked.

12(11)
For *Adonai*, God, is a sun and a shield;
Adonai bestows favor and honor;
he will not withhold anything good
from those whose lives are pure.

13(12)
Adonai-Tzva'ot,
how happy is anyone who trusts in you!

85 1(0) For the leader. A psalm of the sons of Korach:

2(1)
Adonai, you have shown favor to your land;
you have restored the fortunes of Ya'akov,

3(2)
taken away the guilt of your people,
pardoned all their sin,   (*Selah*)

4(3)
withdrawn all your wrath,
turned from your fierce anger.

5(4)
Restore us, God of our salvation,
renounce your displeasure with us.

6(5)
Are you to stay angry with us forever?
Will your fury last through all generations?

7(6)
Won't you revive us again,
so your people can rejoice in you?

8(7)
Show us your grace, *Adonai*;
grant us your salvation.

9(8)
I am listening. What will God, *Adonai*, say?
For he will speak peace to his people,
to his holy ones —
but only if they don't relapse into folly.

10(9)
His salvation is near for those who fear him,
so that glory will be in our land.

11(10)
Grace and truth have met together;
justice and peace have kissed each other.

12(11)
Truth springs up from the earth,
and justice looks down from heaven.

13(12)
Adonai will also grant prosperity;
our land will yield its harvest.

14(13)
Justice will walk before him
and make his footsteps a path.

86[1(0)] A prayer of David:

[(1)]   Listen, *Adonai*, and answer me,
for I am poor and needy.

[2]   Preserve my life, for I am faithful;
save your servant,
who puts his trust in you
because you are my God.

[3]   Take pity on me, *Adonai*,
for I cry to you all day.

[4]   Fill your servant's heart with joy,
for to you, *Adonai*, I lift my heart.

[5]   *Adonai*, you are kind and forgiving,
full of grace toward all who call on you.

[6]   Listen, *Adonai*, to my prayer;
pay attention to my pleading cry.

[7]   On the day of my trouble I am calling on you,
for you will answer me.

[8]   There is none like you among the gods, *Adonai*;
no deeds compare with yours.

[9]   All the nations you have made
will come and bow before you, *Adonai*;
they will honor your name.

[10]   For you are great, and you do wonders;
you alone are God.

[11]   *Adonai*, teach me your way,
so that I can live by your truth;
make me single-hearted,
so that I can fear your name.

[12]   I will thank you, *Adonai* my God,
with my whole heart;
and I will glorify your name forever.

[13]   For your grace toward me is so great!
You have rescued me from the lowest part of Sh'ol.

[14]   God, arrogant men are rising against me,
a gang of brutes is seeking my life,
and to you they pay no attention.

[15]   But you, *Adonai*,
are a merciful, compassionate God,
slow to anger
and rich in grace and truth.

[16]   Turn to me, and show me your favor;
strengthen your servant, save your slave-girl's son.

17   Give me a sign of your favor,
so that those who hate me
will see it and be ashamed,
because you, ADONAI,
have helped and comforted me.

87 ^1(0) A psalm of the sons of Korach. A song:

(1)   On the holy mountains is [the city's] foundation.

2   ADONAI loves the gates of Tziyon
more than all the dwellings in Ya'akov.

3   Glorious things are said about you,
city of God.   (Selah)

4   I count Rahav and Bavel
among those who know me.
Of P'leshet, Tzor and Ethiopia [they will say],
"This one was born there."

5   But of Tziyon it will be said,
"This one and that was born in it,
for the Most High himself establishes it."

6   When he registers the peoples, ADONAI will record,
"This one was born there."   (Selah)

7   Singers and dancers alike say,
"For me, you are the source of everything."

88 ^1(0) A song. A psalm of the sons of Korach. For the leader. Set to "Sickness that Causes Suffering." A *maskil* of Heiman the Ezrachi.

2(1)   ADONAI, God of my salvation,
when I cry out to you in the night,

3(2)   let my prayer come before you,
turn your ear to my cry for help!

4(3)   For I am oversupplied with troubles,
which have brought me to the brink of Sh'ol.

5(4)   I am counted among those going down to the pit,
like a man who is beyond help,

6(5)   left by myself among the dead,
like the slain who lie in the grave —
you no longer remember them;
they are cut off from your care.

7(6)   You plunged me into the bottom of the pit,
into dark places, into the depths.

8(7) Your wrath lies heavily on me;
      your waves crashing over me keep me down.   (*Selah*)
9(8) You separated me from my close friends,
      made me repulsive to them;
      I am caged in, with no escape;
10(9) my eyes grow dim from suffering.

      I call on you, ADONAI, every day;
      I spread out my hands to you.
11(10) Will you perform wonders for the dead?
       Can the ghosts of the dead rise up and praise you?   (*Selah*)
12(11) Will your grace be declared in the grave,
       or your faithfulness in Abaddon?
13(12) Will your wonders be known in the dark,
       or your righteousness in the land of oblivion?

14(13) But I cry out to you, ADONAI;
       my prayer comes before you in the morning.
15(14) So why, ADONAI, do you reject me?
       Why do you hide your face from me?

16(15) Since my youth I have been miserable, close to death;
       I am numb from bearing these terrors of yours.
17(16) Your fierce anger has overwhelmed me,
       your terrors have shriveled me up.
18(17) They surge around me all day like a flood,
       from all sides they close in on me.
19(18) You have made friends and companions shun me;
       the people I know are hidden from me.

89[1(0)] A *maskil* of Eitan the Ezrachi:

2(1) I will sing about ADONAI's acts of grace forever,
     with my mouth proclaim your faithfulness to all generations;
3(2) because I said, "Grace is built to last forever;
     in the heavens themselves you established your faithfulness."

4(3) You said, "I made a covenant with the one I chose,
     I swore to my servant David,
5(4) 'I will establish your dynasty forever,
     build up your throne through all generations.'"   (*Selah*)

6(5) Let the heavens praise your wonders, ADONAI,
     your faithfulness in the assembly of the angels.
7(6) For who in the skies can be compared with ADONAI?
     Which of these gods can rival ADONAI,

8(7)   a God dreaded in the great assembly of the holy ones
         and feared by all around him?

9(8)   *Adonai Elohei-Tzva'ot*!
         Who is as mighty as you, *Yah*?
         Your faithfulness surrounds you.
10(9)   You control the raging of the sea;
         when its waves rear up, you calm them.
11(10)   You crushed Rahav like a carcass;
         with your strong arm you scattered your foes.
12(11)   The heavens are yours, and the earth is yours;
         you founded the world and everything in it.
13(12)   You created north and south;
         Tavor and Hermon take joy in your name.

14(13)   Your arm is mighty, your hand is strong,
         your right hand is lifted high.
15(14)   Righteousness and justice are the foundation of your throne;
         grace and truth attend you.

16(15)   How happy are the people who know the joyful shout!
         They walk in the light of your presence, *Adonai*.
17(16)   They rejoice in your name all day
         and are lifted up by your righteousness,
18(17)   for you yourself are the strength in which they glory.
         Our power grows by pleasing you,
19(18)   for our shield comes from *Adonai* —
         our king is from the Holy One of Isra'el.

20(19)   There was a time when you spoke in a vision;
         you declared to your loyal [prophets],
         "I have given help to a warrior,
         I have raised up someone chosen from the people.
21(20)   I have found David my servant
         and anointed him with my holy oil.
22(21)   My hand will always be with him,
         and my arm will give him strength.
23(22)   No enemy will outwit him,
         no wicked man overcome him.
24(23)   I will crush his foes before him
         and strike down those who hate him.
25(24)   My faithfulness and grace will be with him;
         through my name his power will grow.
26(25)   I will put his hand on the sea
         and his right hand on the rivers.
27(26)   He will call to me, 'You are my father,
         my God, the Rock of my salvation.'

28(27) I will give him the position of firstborn,
        the highest of the kings of the earth.
29(28) I will keep my grace for him forever,
        and in my covenant be faithful with him.
30(29) I will establish his dynasty forever,
        and his throne as long as the heavens last.

31(30) "If his descendants abandon my *Torah*
        and fail to live by my rulings,
32(31) if they profane my regulations
        and don't obey my *mitzvot*,
33(32) I will punish their disobedience with the rod
        and their guilt with lashes.
34(33) But I won't withdraw my grace from him
        or be false to my faithfulness.
35(34) I will not profane my covenant
        or change what my lips have spoken.
36(35) I have sworn by my holiness once and for all;
        I will not lie to David —
37(36) his dynasty will last forever,
        his throne like the sun before me.
38(37) It will be established forever, like the moon,
        which remains a faithful witness in the sky."   (*Selah*)

39(38) But you spurned your anointed one,
        rejected and vented your rage on him.
40(39) You renounced the covenant with your servant
        and defiled his crown in the dust.
41(40) You broke through all his defenses
        and left his strongholds in ruins.
42(41) All who pass by plunder him;
        he is an object of scorn to his neighbors.
43(42) You raised up the right hand of his foes
        and made all his enemies rejoice.
44(43) You drive back his drawn sword
        and fail to support him in battle.
45(44) You brought an end to his splendor
        and hurled his throne to the ground.
46(45) You cut short the days of his youth
        and covered him with shame.   (*Selah*)

47(46) How long, A<small>DONAI</small>? Will you hide yourself forever?
        How long will your fury burn like fire?
48(47) Remember how little time I have!
        Was it for no purpose that you created all humanity?
49(48) Who can live and not see death?
        Who can save himself from the power of the grave?   (*Selah*)

50(49) Where, *Adonai*, are the acts of grace you once did,
        those which, in your faithfulness, you swore to David?
51(50) Remember, *Adonai*, the taunts hurled at your servants,
        which I carry in my heart [from] so many peoples!
52(51) Your enemies, ADONAI, have flung their taunts,
        flung them in the footsteps of your anointed one.

53(52) Blessed be ADONAI forever.
        Amen. Amen.

Book IV: Psalms 90–106

90 ¹⁽⁰⁾ A prayer of Moshe the man of God:

(1) *Adonai*, you have been our dwelling place
     in every generation.
2   Before the mountains were born,
     before you had formed the earth and the world,
     from eternity past to eternity future
     you are God.

3   You bring frail mortals to the point of being crushed,
     then say, "People, repent!"
4   For from your viewpoint a thousand years
     are merely like yesterday or a night watch.
5   When you sweep them away, they become like sleep;
     by morning they are like growing grass,
6   growing and flowering in the morning,
     but by evening cut down and dried up.

7   For we are destroyed by your anger,
     overwhelmed by your wrath.
8   You have placed our faults before you,
     our secret sins in the full light of your presence.

9   All our days ebb away under your wrath;
     our years die away like a sigh.
10   The span of our life is seventy years,
     or if we are strong, eighty;
     yet at best it is toil and sorrow,
     over in a moment, and then we are gone.

11   Who grasps the power of your anger and wrath
     to the degree that the fear due you should inspire?

12   So teach us to count our days,
     so that we will become wise.

13   Return, ADONAI! How long must it go on?
     Take pity on your servants!
14   Fill us at daybreak with your love,
     so that we can sing for joy as long as we live.
15   Let our joy last as long as the time you made us suffer,
     for as many years as we experienced trouble.

16   Show your deeds to your servants
     and your glory to their children.
17   May the favor of *Adonai* our God be on us,
     prosper for us all the work that we do —
     yes, prosper the work that we do.

91 1   You who live in the shelter of *'Elyon*,
     who spend your nights in the shadow of *Shaddai*,
2   who say to ADONAI, "My refuge! My fortress!
     My God, in whom I trust!" —
3   he will rescue you from the trap of the hunter
     and from the plague of calamities;
4   he will cover you with his pinions,
     and under his wings you will find refuge;
     his truth is a shield and protection.

5   You will not fear the terrors of night
     or the arrow that flies by day,
6   or the plague that roams in the dark,
     or the scourge that wreaks havoc at noon.
7   A thousand may fall at your side,
     ten thousand at your right hand;
     but it won't come near you.
8   Only keep your eyes open,
     and you will see how the wicked are punished.

9   For you have made ADONAI, the Most High,
     who is my refuge, your dwelling-place.
10   No disaster will happen to you,
     no calamity will come near your tent;
11   for he will order his angels to care for you
     and guard you wherever you go.
12   They will carry you in their hands,
     so that you won't trip on a stone.
13   You will tread down lions and snakes,
     young lions and serpents you will trample underfoot.

14 "Because he loves me, I will rescue him;
    because he knows my name, I will protect him.
15 He will call on me, and I will answer him.
    I will be with him when he is in trouble.
    I will extricate him and bring him honor.
16 I will satisfy him with long life
    and show him my salvation."

92 $^{1(0)}$ A psalm. A song for *Shabbat*:

2(1) It is good to give thanks to A$_{DONAI}$
      and sing praises to your name, *'Elyon*,
3(2) to tell in the morning about your grace
      and at night about your faithfulness,
4(3) to the music of a ten-stringed [harp] and a lute,
      with the melody sounding on a lyre.

5(4) For, A$_{DONAI}$, what you do makes me happy;
      I take joy in what your hands have made.
6(5) How great are your deeds, A$_{DONAI}$!
      How very deep your thoughts!

7(6) Stupid people can't know,
      fools don't understand,
8(7) that when the wicked sprout like grass,
      and all who do evil prosper,
      it is so that they can be eternally destroyed,
9(8) while you, A$_{DONAI}$, are exalted forever.

10(9) For your enemies, A$_{DONAI}$,
       your enemies will perish;
       all evildoers will be scattered.
11(10) But you have given me
       the strength of a wild bull;
       you anoint me with fresh olive oil.
12(11) My eyes have gazed with pleasure on my enemies' ruin,
       my ears have delighted in the fall of my foes.

13(12) The righteous will flourish like a palm tree,
       they will grow like a cedar in the L'vanon.
14(13) Planted in the house of A$_{DONAI}$,
       they will flourish in the courtyards of our God.
15(14) Even in old age they will be vigorous,
       still full of sap, still bearing fruit,
16(15) proclaiming that A$_{DONAI}$ is upright,
       my Rock, in whom there is no wrong.

93¹ *Adonai* is king, robed in majesty;
       Adonai is robed, girded with strength.
       The world is well established;
       it cannot be moved.
²   Your throne was established long ago;
       you have existed forever.
³   *Adonai*, the deep is raising up,
       the deep is raising up its voice,
       the deep is raising its crashing waves.
⁴   More than the sound of rushing waters
       or the mighty breakers of the sea,
       Adonai on high is mighty.
⁵   Your instructions are very sure;
       holiness befits your house,
       Adonai, for all time to come.

94¹ God of vengeance, *Adonai*!
       God of vengeance, appear!
²   Assert yourself as judge of the earth!
       Pay back the proud as they deserve!

³   How long are the wicked, *Adonai*,
       how long are the wicked to triumph?
⁴   They pour out insolent words,
       they go on bragging, all these evildoers.

⁵   They crush your people, *Adonai*,
       they oppress your heritage.
⁶   They kill widows and strangers
       and murder the fatherless.

⁷   They say, "*Yah* isn't looking;
       the God of Ya'akov won't notice."
⁸   Take notice, yourselves, you boors among the people!
       You fools, when will you understand?
⁹   Will the one who planted the ear not hear?
       Will the one who formed the eye not see?
¹⁰   Will the one who disciplines nations not correct them?
       Will the teacher of humanity not know?
¹¹   *Adonai* understands that people's thoughts
       are merely a puff of wind.

¹²   How happy the man whom you correct, *Yah*,
       whom you teach from your *Torah*,
¹³   giving him respite from days of trouble,
       till a pit is dug for the wicked!

¹⁴ For *Adonai* will not desert his people,
he will not abandon his heritage.
¹⁵ Justice will once again become righteous,
and all the upright in heart will follow it.

¹⁶ Who will champion my cause against the wicked?
Who will stand up for me against evildoers?

¹⁷ If *Adonai* hadn't helped me,
I would soon have dwelt in the land of silence.
¹⁸ When I said, "My foot is slipping!"
your grace, *Adonai*, supported me.
¹⁹ When my cares within me are many,
your comforts cheer me up.

²⁰ Can unjust judges be allied with you,
those producing wrong in the name of law?
²¹ They band together against the righteous
and condemn the innocent to death.

²² But *Adonai* has become my stronghold,
my God is my rock of refuge.
²³ But he repays them as their guilt deserves;
he will cut them off with their own evil;
Adonai our God will cut them off.

95 ¹ Come, let's sing to *Adonai*!
Let's shout for joy to the Rock of our salvation!
² Let's come into his presence with thanksgiving;
let's shout for joy to him with songs of praise.

³ For *Adonai* is a great God,
a great king greater than all gods.
⁴ He holds the depths of the earth in his hands;
the mountain peaks too belong to him.
⁵ The sea is his — he made it —
and his hands shaped the dry land.

⁶ Come, let's bow down and worship;
let's kneel before *Adonai* who made us.
⁷ For he is our God, and we are the people
in his pasture, the sheep in his care.

If only today you would listen to his voice:
⁸ "Don't harden your hearts, as you did at M'rivah,
as you did on that day at Massah in the desert,

⁹   when your fathers put me to the test;
       they challenged me, even though they saw my work.
¹⁰   For forty years I loathed that generation;
       I said, 'This is a people whose hearts go astray,
       they don't understand how I do things.'
¹¹   Therefore I swore in my anger
       that they would not enter my rest."

96 ¹   Sing to Aᴅᴏɴᴀɪ a new song!
          Sing to Aᴅᴏɴᴀɪ, all the earth!
²   Sing to Aᴅᴏɴᴀɪ, bless his name!
          Proclaim his victory day after day!
³   Declare his glory among the nations,
          his wonders among all peoples!

⁴   For Aᴅᴏɴᴀɪ is great, and greatly to be praised;
          he is to be feared more than all gods.
⁵   For all the gods of the peoples are idols,
          but Aᴅᴏɴᴀɪ made the heavens.
⁶   In his presence are honor and majesty;
          in his sanctuary, strength and splendor.

⁷   Give Aᴅᴏɴᴀɪ his due, you families from the peoples;
          give Aᴅᴏɴᴀɪ his due of glory and strength;
⁸   give Aᴅᴏɴᴀɪ the glory due to his name;
          bring an offering, and enter his courtyards.
⁹   Worship Aᴅᴏɴᴀɪ in holy splendor;
          tremble before him, all the earth!
¹⁰   Say among the nations, "Aᴅᴏɴᴀɪ is king!"
          The world is firmly established, immovable.
          He will judge the peoples fairly.

¹¹   Let the heavens rejoice; let the earth be glad;
          let the sea roar, and everything in it;
¹²   let the fields exult and all that is in them.
          Then all the trees in the forest will sing
¹³   before Aᴅᴏɴᴀɪ, because he has come,
          he has come to judge the earth;
          he will judge the world rightly
          and the peoples with his faithfulness.

97 ¹   Aᴅᴏɴᴀɪ is king, let the earth rejoice,
          let the many coasts and islands be glad.
²   Clouds and thick darkness surround him;
          righteousness and justice are the foundation of his throne.

³ Fire goes before him,
  setting ablaze his foes on every side.
⁴ His flashes of lightning light up the world;
  the earth sees it and trembles.
⁵ The mountains melt like wax at the presence of ADONAI,
  at the presence of the Lord of all the earth.
⁶ The heavens declare his righteousness,
  and all the peoples see his glory.

⁷ All who worship images will be put to shame,
  those who make their boast in worthless idols.
  Bow down to him, all you gods!
⁸ Tziyon hears and is glad, ADONAI;
  the daughters of Y'hudah rejoice at your rulings.
⁹ For you, ADONAI, most high over all the earth,
  you are exalted far above all gods.

¹⁰ You who love ADONAI, hate evil!
   He keeps his faithful servants safe.
   He rescues them from the power of the wicked.
¹¹ Light is sown for the righteous
   and joy for the upright in heart.
¹² Rejoice in ADONAI, you righteous;
   and give thanks on recalling his holiness.

98 ¹⁽⁰⁾ A psalm:

⁽¹⁾ Sing a new song to ADONAI,
    because he has done wonders.
    His right hand, his holy arm
    have won him victory.
² ADONAI has made known his victory;
  revealed his vindication in full view of the nations,
³ remembered his grace and faithfulness
  to the house of Isra'el.
  All the ends of the earth have seen
  the victory of our God.

⁴ Shout for joy to ADONAI, all the earth!
  Break forth, sing for joy, sing praises!
⁵ Sing praises to ADONAI with the lyre,
  with the lyre and melodious music!
⁶ With trumpets and the sound of the *shofar*,
  shout for joy before the king, ADONAI!
⁷ Let the sea roar, and everything in it;
  the world, and those living in it.

8 Let the floods clap their hands;
  let the mountains sing together for joy
9 before ADONAI, for he has come to judge the earth;
  he will judge the world rightly and the peoples fairly.

99 1 ADONAI is king; let the peoples tremble.
  He sits enthroned on the k'ruvim; let the earth shake!
2 ADONAI is great in Tziyon;
  he is high above all the peoples.

3 Let them praise your great and fearsome name (he is holy):
4 "Mighty king who loves justice, you established
  fairness, justice and righteousness in Ya'akov."

5 Exalt ADONAI our God!
  Prostrate yourselves at his footstool (he is holy).

6 Moshe and Aharon among his cohanim
  and Sh'mu'el among those who call on his name
  called on ADONAI, and he answered them.
7 He spoke to them in the column of cloud;
  they kept his instructions and the law that he gave them.
8 ADONAI our God, you answered them.
  To them you were a forgiving God,
  although you took vengeance on their wrongdoings.

9 Exalt ADONAI our God,
  bow down toward his holy mountain,
  for ADONAI our God is holy!

100 (1) A psalm of thanksgiving:

(1) Shout for joy to ADONAI, all the earth!
2 Serve ADONAI with gladness.
  Enter his presence with joyful songs.

3 Be aware that ADONAI is God;
  it is he who made us; and we are his,
  his people, the flock in his pasture.

4 Enter his gates with thanksgiving,
  enter his courtyards with praise;
  give thanks to him, and bless his name.
5 For ADONAI is good, his grace continues forever,
  and his faithfulness lasts through all generations.

101 $^{1(0)}$ A psalm of David:

$^{(1)}$ I am singing of grace and justice;
I am singing to you, *Adonai*.

^{2} I will follow the path of integrity;
when will you come to me?
I will run my life with a sincere heart
inside my own house.

^{3} I will not allow before my eyes
any shameful thing.
I hate those who act crookedly;
what they do does not attract me.

^{4} Deviousness will depart from me;
I will not tolerate evil.

^{5} If someone slanders another in secret,
I will cut him off.
Haughty eyes and proud hearts
I cannot abide.

^{6} I look to the faithful of the land,
so that they can be my companions;
those who live lives of integrity
can be servants of mine.

^{7} No deceitful person can live in my house;
no liar can be my advisor.

^{8} Every morning I will destroy
all the wicked of the land,
cutting off all evildoers
from the city of *Adonai*.

102 $^{1(0)}$ Prayer of a sufferer overcome by weakness and pouring out his complaint before *Adonai*:

$^{2(1)}$ *Adonai*, hear my prayer!
Let my cry for help reach you!

$^{3(2)}$ Don't hide your face from me
when I am in such distress!
Turn your ear toward me;
when I call, be quick to reply!

$^{4(3)}$ For my days are vanishing like smoke,
my bones are burning like a furnace.

$^{5(4)}$ I am stricken and withered like grass;
I forget to eat my food.

$^{6(5)}$ Because of my loud groaning,
I am just skin and bones.

7(6)   I am like a great owl in the desert,
       I've become like an owl in the ruins.
8(7)   I lie awake and become
       like a bird alone on the roof.

9(8)   My enemies taunt me all day long;
       mad with rage, they make my name a curse.
10(9) For I have been eating ashes like bread
       and mingling tears with my drink
11(10) because of your furious anger,
       since you picked me up just to toss me aside.
12(11) My days decline like an evening shadow;
       I am drying up like grass.

13(12) But you, ADONAI, are enthroned forever;
       your renown will endure through all generations.
14(13) You will arise and take pity on Tziyon,
       for the time has come to have mercy on her;
       the time determined has come.
15(14) For your servants love her very stones;
       they take pity even on her dust.

16(15) The nations will fear the name of ADONAI
       and all the kings on earth your glory,
17(16) when ADONAI has rebuilt Tziyon,
       and shows himself in his glory,
18(17) when he has heeded the plea of the poor
       and not despised their prayer.
19(18) May this be put on record for a future generation;
       may a people yet to be created praise ADONAI.

20(19) For he has looked down from the height of his sanctuary;
       from heaven ADONAI surveys the earth
21(20) to listen to the sighing of the prisoner,
       to set free those who are sentenced to death,
22(21) to proclaim the name of ADONAI in Tziyon
       and his praise in Yerushalayim
23(22) when peoples and kingdoms have been gathered together
       to serve ADONAI.

24(23) He has broken my strength in midcourse,
       he has cut short my days.
25(24) I plead, "God, your years last through all generations;
       so don't take me away when my life is half over!

26(25) "In the beginning, you laid the foundations of the earth;
       heaven is the work of your hands.

27(26)　They will vanish, but you will remain;
　　　like clothing, they will all grow old;
　　　yes, you will change them like clothing,
　　　and they will pass away.
28(27)　But you remain the same,
　　　and your years will never end.
29(28)　The children of your servants will live securely
　　　and their descendants be established in your presence."

103 ¹⁽⁰⁾ By David:

(1)　Bless Adonai, my soul!
　　　Everything in me, bless his holy name!
2　Bless Adonai, my soul,
　　　and forget none of his benefits!

3　He forgives all your offenses,
　　　he heals all your diseases,
4　he redeems your life from the pit,
　　　he surrounds you with grace and compassion,
5　he contents you with good as long as you live,
　　　so that your youth is renewed like an eagle's.

6　Adonai brings vindication and justice
　　　to all who are oppressed.
7　He made his ways known to Moshe,
　　　his mighty deeds to the people of Isra'el.
8　Adonai is merciful and compassionate,
　　　slow to anger and rich in grace.
9　He will not always accuse,
　　　he will not keep his anger forever.
10　He has not treated us as our sins deserve
　　　or paid us back for our offenses,
11　because his mercy toward those who fear him
　　　is as far above earth as heaven.
12　He has removed our sins from us
　　　as far as the east is from the west.

13　Just as a father has compassion on his children,
　　　Adonai has compassion on those who fear him.
14　For he understands how we are made,
　　　he remembers that we are dust.
15　Yes, a human being's days are like grass,
　　　he sprouts like a flower in the countryside —
16　but when the wind sweeps over, it's gone;
　　　and its place knows it no more.

17 But the mercy of *Adonai* on those who fear him
    is from eternity past to eternity future,
    and his righteousness extends
    to his children's children,
18 provided they keep his covenant
    and remember to follow his precepts.

19 *Adonai* has established his throne in heaven;
    his kingly power rules everything.
20 Bless *Adonai*, you angels of his,
    you mighty warriors who obey his word,
    who carry out his orders!
21 Bless *Adonai*, all his troops,
    who serve him and do what he wants!
22 Bless *Adonai*, all his works,
    in every place where he rules!
    Bless *Adonai*, my soul!

104 1 Bless *Adonai*, my soul!
    Adonai, my God, you are very great;
    you are clothed with glory and majesty,
2   wrapped in light as with a robe.
    You spread out the heavens like a curtain,
3   you laid the beams of your palace on the water.
    You make the clouds your chariot,
    you ride on the wings of the wind.
4   You make winds your messengers,
    fiery flames your servants.

5   You fixed the earth on its foundations,
    never to be moved.
6   You covered it with the deep like a garment;
    the waters stood above the mountains.
7   At your rebuke they fled;
    at the sound of your thunder they rushed away,
8   flowing over hills, pouring into valleys,
    down to the place you had fixed for them.
9   You determined a boundary they could not cross;
    they were never to cover the earth again.

10 You make springs gush forth in the *vadis*;
    they flow between the hills,
11 supplying water to all the wild animals;
    the wild donkeys quench their thirst.
12 On their banks the birds of the air build their nests;
    among the branches they sing.

13 You water the mountains from your palace;
the earth is satisfied with how you provide —
14 you grow grass for the cattle;
and for people you grow the plants they need
to bring forth bread from the earth,
15 wine that gladdens the human heart,
oil to make faces glow,
and food to sustain their strength.

16 ADONAI's trees are satisfied —
the cedars of the L'vanon, which he has planted.
17 In them sparrows build their nests,
while storks live in the fir trees.
18 For the wild goats there are the high mountains,
while the coneys find refuge in the rocks.

19 You made the moon to mark the seasons,
and the sun knows when to set.
20 You bring darkness, and it is night,
the time when all forest animals prowl.
21 The young lions roar after their prey
and seek their food from God.
22 The sun rises, they slink away
and lie down to rest in their dens;
23 while people go out to their work,
laboring on till evening.

24 What variety there is in your works, ADONAI!
How many [of them there are]!
In wisdom you have made them all;
the earth is full of your creations.

25 Look at the sea, so great, so wide!
It teems with countless creatures,
living beings, both large and small.
26 The ships are there, sailing to and fro;
Livyatan, which you formed to play there.

27 All of them look to you
to give them their food when they need it.
28 When you give it to them, they gather it;
when you open your hand, they are well satisfied.
29 If you hide your face, they vanish;
if you hold back their breath, they perish
and return to their dust.
30 If you send out your breath, they are created,
and you renew the face of the earth.

31 May the glory of *Adonai* last forever!
May *Adonai* rejoice in his works!
32 When he looks at the earth, it trembles;
when he touches the mountains, they pour out smoke.
33 I will sing to *Adonai* as long as I live,
sing praise to my God all my life.
34 May my musings be pleasing to him;
I will rejoice in *Adonai*.
35 May sinners vanish from the earth
and the wicked be no more!
Bless *Adonai*, my soul!

Halleluyah!

105 1 Give thanks to *Adonai*! Call on his name!
Make his deeds known among the peoples.
2 Sing to him, sing praises to him,
talk about all his wonders.
3 Glory in his holy name;
let those seeking *Adonai* have joyful hearts.
4 Seek *Adonai* and his strength;
always seek his presence.
5 Remember the wonders he has done,
his signs and his spoken rulings.

6 You descendants of Avraham his servant,
you offspring of Ya'akov, his chosen ones,
7 he is *Adonai* our God!
His rulings are everywhere on earth.
8 He remembers his covenant forever,
the word he commanded to a thousand generations,
9 the covenant he made with Avraham,
the oath he swore to Yitz'chak,
10 and established as a law for Ya'akov,
for Isra'el as an everlasting covenant:
11 "To you I will give the land of Kena'an
as your allotted heritage."

12 When they were but few in number,
and not only few, but aliens there too,
13 wandering from nation to nation,
from this kingdom to that people,
14 he allowed no one to oppress them.
Yes, for their sakes he rebuked even kings:
15 "Don't touch my anointed ones
or do my prophets harm!"

16 · He called down famine on the land,
    broke off all their food supply,
17   but sent a man ahead of them —
    Yosef, who was sold as a slave.
18   They shackled his feet with chains,
    and they bound him in irons;
19   until the time when his word proved true,
    God's utterance kept testing him.
20   The king sent and had him released,
    the ruler of peoples set him free;
21   he made him lord of his household,
    in charge of all he owned,
22   correcting his officers as he saw fit
    and teaching his counselors wisdom.

23   Then Isra'el too came into Egypt,
    Ya'akov lived as an alien in the land of Ham.
24   There God made his people very fruitful,
    made them too numerous for their foes,
25   whose hearts he turned to hate his people,
    and treat his servants unfairly.

26   He sent his servant Moshe
    and Aharon, whom he had chosen.
27   They worked his signs among them,
    his wonders in the land of Ham.

28   He sent darkness, and the land grew dark;
    they did not defy his word.

29   He turned their water into blood
    and caused their fish to die.

30   Their land swarmed with frogs,
    even in the royal chambers.

31   He spoke, and there came swarms of insects
    and lice throughout their land.

32   He gave them hail instead of rain,
    with fiery [lightning] throughout their land.
33   He struck their vines and fig trees,
    shattering trees all over their country.

34   He spoke, and locusts came,
    also grasshoppers without number;
35   they ate up everything green in their land,
    devoured the fruit of their ground.

36 He struck down all the firstborn in their land,
the firstfruits of all their strength.

37 Then he led his people out,
laden with silver and gold;
among his tribes not one stumbled.
38 Egypt was happy to have them leave,
because fear of [Isra'el] had seized them.

39 He spread out a cloud to screen them off
and fire to give them light at night.
40 When they asked, he brought them quails
and satisfied them with food from heaven.

41 He split a rock, and water gushed out,
flowing as a river over the dry ground,
42 for he remembered his holy promise
to his servant Avraham.

43 He led out his people with joy,
his chosen ones with singing.
44 Then he gave them the lands of the nations,
and they possessed what peoples had toiled to produce,
45 in order to obey his laws
and follow his teachings.

Halleluyah!

106¹ *Halleluyah!*

Give thanks to A*DONAI*, for he is good,
for his grace continues forever.
2 Who can express A*DONAI*'s mighty doings
or proclaim in full his praise?
3 How happy are those who act justly,
who always do what is right!

4 Remember me, A*DONAI*, when you show favor to your people,
keep me in mind when you save them;
5 so I can see how well things are going
with those whom you have chosen,
so that I can rejoice in your nation's joy,
and glory in your heritage.

6 Together with our ancestors, we have sinned,
done wrong, acted wickedly.

7   Our ancestors in Egypt failed to grasp
    the meaning of your wonders.
    They didn't keep in mind your great deeds of grace
    but rebelled at the sea, at the Sea of Suf.

8   Yet he saved them for his own name's sake,
    to make known his mighty power.

9   He rebuked the Sea of Suf, and it dried up;
    he led them through its depths as through a desert.

10   He saved them from hostile hands,
    redeemed them from the power of the foe.

11   The water closed over their adversaries;
    not one of them was left.

12   Then they believed his words,
    and they sang his praise.

13   But soon they forgot his deeds
    and wouldn't wait for his counsel.

14   In the desert they gave way to insatiable greed;
    in the wastelands they put God to the test.

15   He gave them what they wanted
    but sent meagerness into their souls.

16   In the camp they were jealous of Moshe
    and Aharon, ADONAI's holy one.

17   The earth opened up and swallowed Datan
    and closed over Aviram's allies.

18   A fire blazed out against that group,
    the flames consumed the wicked.

19   In Horev they fashioned a calf,
    they worshipped a cast metal image.

20   Thus they exchanged their Glory
    for the image of an ox that eats grass!

21   They forgot God, who had saved them,
    who had done great things in Egypt,

22   wonders in the land of Ham,
    fearsome deeds by the Sea of Suf.

23   Therefore he said that he would destroy them,
    [and he would have,] had not Moshe his chosen one
    stood before him in the breach
    to turn back his destroying fury.

24   Next, they rejected the beautiful land,
    they didn't trust his promise;

25   and they complained in their tents,
    they didn't obey ADONAI.

26 Therefore, raising his hand, he swore to them
that he would strike them down in the desert
27 and strike down their descendants among the nations,
dispersing them in foreign lands.

28 Now they joined themselves to Ba'al-P'or
and ate meat sacrificed to dead things.
29 Thus they provoked him to anger with their deeds,
so that a plague broke out among them.
30 Then Pinchas stood up and executed judgment;
so the plague was checked.
31 That was credited to him as righteousness,
through all generations forever.

32 They angered him at the M'rivah Spring,
and Moshe suffered on their account;
33 for when they embittered his spirit,
[Moshe] spoke up without thinking.

34 They failed to destroy the peoples,
as Adonai had ordered them to do,
35 but mingled with the nations
and learned to follow their ways.
36 They went on to serve their idols,
which became a snare for them.
37 They even sacrificed their sons
and their daughters to demons.
38 Yes, they shed innocent blood,
the blood of their own sons and daughters,
whom they sacrificed to Kena'an's false gods,
polluting the land with blood.
39 Thus they were defiled by their deeds;
they prostituted themselves by their actions.

40 For this Adonai's fury blazed up against his people,
and he detested his heritage.
41 He handed them over to the power of the nations,
and those who hated them ruled over them.
42 Their enemies oppressed them
and kept them in subjection to their power.
43 Many times [God] rescued them,
but they kept making plans to rebel.
Thus they were brought low
by their own wrongdoing.

44 Still he took pity on their distress
whenever he heard their cry.

45 For their sakes he kept in mind his covenant
and in his limitless grace relented,
46 causing them to be treated with compassion
by all who had taken them captive.

47 Save us, *Adonai* our God!
Gather us from among the nations,
so that we can thank your holy name
and glory in praising you.

48 Blessed be *Adonai*, the God of Isra'el,
from eternity past to eternity future.
Now let all the people say,
"*Amen*! *Halleluyah*!"

Book V: Psalms 107–150

107 ¹ Give thanks to *Adonai*, for he is good,
for his grace continues forever.
2 Let those redeemed by *Adonai* say it,
those he redeemed from the power of the foe.
3 He gathered them from the lands,
from the east and from the west,
from the north and from the sea.

4 They wandered in the desert, on paths through the wastes,
without finding any inhabited city.
5 They were hungry and thirsty,
their life was ebbing away.

6 In their trouble they cried to *Adonai*,
and he rescued them from their distress.
7 He led them by a direct path
to a city where they could live.

8 Let them give thanks to *Adonai* for his grace,
for his wonders bestowed on humanity!
9 For he has satisfied the hungry,
filled the starving with that which is good.

10 Some lived in darkness, in death-dark gloom,
bound in misery and iron chains,
11 because they defied God's word,
scorned the counsel of the Most High.

12 So he humbled their hearts by hard labor;
when they stumbled, no one came to their aid.

13 In their trouble they cried to ADONAI,
and he rescued them from their distress.
14 He led them from darkness, from death-dark gloom,
shattering their chains.

15 Let them give thanks to ADONAI for his grace,
for his wonders bestowed on humanity!
16 For he shattered bronze doors
and cut through iron bars.

17 There were foolish people who suffered affliction
because of their crimes and sins;
18 they couldn't stand to eat anything;
they were near the gates of death.

19 In their trouble they cried to ADONAI,
and he rescued them from their distress;
20 he sent his word and healed them,
he delivered them from destruction.

21 Let them give thanks to ADONAI for his grace,
for his wonders bestowed on humanity!
22 Let them offer sacrifices of thanksgiving
and proclaim his great deeds with songs of joy.

23 Those who go down to the sea in ships,
plying their trade on the great ocean,
24 saw the works of ADONAI,
his wonders in the deep.

25 For at his word the storm-wind arose,
lifting up towering waves.
26 The sailors were raised up to the sky,
then plunged into the depths.
At the danger, their courage failed them,
27 they reeled and staggered like drunk men,
and all their skill was swallowed up.

28 In their trouble they cried to ADONAI,
and he rescued them from their distress.
29 He silenced the storm and stilled its waves,
30 and they rejoiced as the sea grew calm.
Then he brought them safely
to their desired port.

113

31 Let them give thanks to *Adonai* for his grace,
for his wonders bestowed on humanity!
32 Let them extol him in the assembly of the people
and praise him in the leaders' council.

33 He turns rivers into desert,
flowing springs into thirsty ground,
34 productive land into salt flats,
because the people living there are so wicked.

35 But he also turns desert into pools of water,
dry land into flowing springs;
36 there he gives the hungry a home,
and they build a city to live in;
37 there they sow fields and plant vineyards,
which yield an abundant harvest.

38 He blesses them, their numbers grow,
and he doesn't let their livestock decrease.
39 When their numbers fall, and they grow weak,
because of oppression, disaster and sorrow,
40 he pours contempt on princes
and leaves them to wander in trackless wastes.

41 But the needy he raises up from their distress
and increases their families like sheep.
42 When the upright see this, they rejoice;
while the wicked are reduced to silence.
43 Let whoever is wise observe these things
and consider *Adonai*'s loving deeds.

108 ¹⁽⁰⁾ A song. A psalm of David:

2(1) My heart is steadfast, God.
I will sing and make music with my glory.
3(2) Awake, lute and lyre!
I will awaken the dawn.
4(3) I will thank you, *Adonai*, among the peoples;
I will make music to you among the nations.
5(4) For your grace is great, above heaven,
and your truth, all the way to the skies.

6(5) Be exalted, God, above heaven!
May your glory be over all the earth,
7(6) in order that those you love can be rescued;
so save with your right hand, and answer me!

8(7) God in his holiness spoke,
and I took joy [in his promise]:
"I will divide Sh'khem
and determine the shares in the Sukkot Valley.
9(8) Gil'ad is mine and M'nasheh mine,
Efrayim my helmet, Y'hudah my scepter.
10(9) Mo'av is my washpot; on Edom I throw my shoe;
Over P'leshet I shout in triumph."

11(10) Who will bring me into the fortified city?
Who will lead me to Edom?
12(11) God, have you rejected us?
You don't go out with our armies, God.
13(12) Help us against our enemy,
for human help is worthless.
14(13) With God's help we will fight valiantly,
for he will trample our enemies.

109 1(0) For the leader. A psalm of David:

(1) God, whom I praise, don't remain silent!
2 For wicked and deceitful men
have opened their mouths against me,
spoken against me with lying tongues,
3 surrounded me with hateful words,
and attacked me without cause.

4 In return for my love they became my accusers,
even though I prayed for them.
5 They repay me evil for good
and hatred for my love.

6 [They say,] "Appoint a wicked man over him,
may an accuser stand at his right.
7 When he is tried, let him be found guilty,
may even his plea be counted a sin.
8 May his days be few,
may someone else take his position.
9 May his children be fatherless
and his wife a widow.
10 May his children be wandering beggars,
foraging for food from their ruined homes.
11 May creditors seize all he owns
and strangers make off with his earnings.
12 May no one treat him kindly,
and may no one take pity on his orphaned children.

115

13   May his posterity be cut off;
    may his name be erased within a generation.

14   May the wrongs of his ancestors be remembered by *Adonai*,
    and may the sin of his mother not be erased;

15   may they always be before *Adonai*,
    so he can cut off all memory of them from the earth.

16   For he did not remember to show kindness
    but hounded the downtrodden, the poor
    and the brokenhearted to death.

17   He loved cursing; may it recoil on him!
    He didn't like blessing; may it stay far from him!

18   He clothed himself with cursing
    as routinely as with his coat.
    May it enter inside him as easily as water,
    as easily as oil into his bones.

19   May it cling to him like the coat he wears,
    like the belt he wraps around himself."

20   This is what my adversaries want *Adonai* to do,
    those who speak evil against me.

21   But you, God, *Adonai*,
    treat me as your name demands;
    rescue me, because your grace is good.

22   For I am poor and needy,
    and my heart within me is wounded.

23   Like a lengthening evening shadow, I am gone;
    I am shaken off like a locust.

24   My knees are weak from lack of food,
    my flesh wastes away for lack of nourishment.

25   I have become the object of their taunts;
    when they see me, they shake their heads.

26   Help me, *Adonai*, my God!
    Save me, in keeping with your grace;

27   so that they will know that this comes from your hand,
    that you, *Adonai*, have done it.

28   Let them go on cursing;
    but you, bless!
    When they attack, let them be put to shame;
    but let your servant rejoice.

29   Let my adversaries be clothed with confusion,
    let them wear their own shame like a robe.

30   I will eagerly thank *Adonai* with my mouth,
    I will praise him right there in the crowd,

31   because he stands alongside a needy person
    to defend him from unjust accusers.

110 [1(0)] A psalm of David:

[1] *Adonai* says to my Lord,
"Sit at my right hand,
until I make your enemies
your footstool."

[2] *Adonai* will send your powerful scepter
out from Tziyon,
so that you will rule over
your enemies around you.
[3] On the day your forces mobilize,
your people willingly offer themselves
in holy splendors from the womb of the dawn;
the dew of your youth is yours.

[4] *Adonai* has sworn it,
and he will never retract —
"You are a *cohen* forever,
to be compared with Malki-Tzedek."

[5] Adonai at your right hand
will shatter kings on the day of his anger.
[6] He will pass judgment among the nations,
filling it with dead bodies;
he will shatter heads
throughout an extensive territory.
[7] He will drink from a stream as he goes on his way;
therefore he will hold his head high.

111 [1] *Halleluyah*!

I will wholeheartedly give thanks to *Adonai*
in the council of the upright and in the assembly.
[2] The deeds of *Adonai* are great,
greatly desired by all who enjoy them.
[3] His work is full of majesty and splendor,
and his righteousness continues forever.
[4] He has gained renown for his wonders.
Adonai is merciful and compassionate.
[5] He gives food to those who fear him.
He remembers his covenant forever.
[6] He shows his people how powerfully he works
by giving them the nations as their heritage.
[7] The works of his hands are truth and justice;
all his precepts can be trusted.

8   They have been established forever and ever,
to be carried out truly and honestly.
9   He sent redemption to his people
and decreed that his covenant should last forever.
His name is holy and fearsome —
10   the first and foremost point of wisdom is the fear of *ADONAI*;
all those living by it gain good common sense.
His praise stands forever.

112 1   *Halleluyah!*

How happy is anyone who fears *ADONAI*,
who greatly delights in his *mitzvot*.
2   His descendants will be powerful on earth,
a blessed generation of upright people.
3   Wealth and riches are in his house,
and his righteousness stands forever.

4   To the upright he shines like a light in the dark,
merciful, compassionate and righteous.
5   Things go well with the person who is merciful and lends,
who conducts his affairs with fairness;
6   for he will never be moved.
The righteous will be remembered forever.

7   He will not be frightened by bad news;
he remains steady, trusting in *ADONAI*.
8   His heart is set firm, he will not be afraid,
till finally he looks in triumph at his enemies.
9   He distributes freely, he gives to the poor;
his righteousness stands forever.

His power will be increased honorably.
10   The wicked will be angry when they see this;
they will gnash their teeth and waste away,
the desires of the wicked will come to nothing.

113 1   *Halleluyah!*

Servants of *ADONAI*, give praise!
Give praise to the name of *ADONAI*!
2   Blessed be the name of *ADONAI*
from this moment on and forever!
3   From sunrise until sunset
ADONAI's name is to be praised.

⁴   *Adonai* is high above all nations,
   his glory above the heavens.
⁵   Who is like *Adonai* our God,
   seated in the heights,
⁶   humbling himself to look
   on heaven and on earth.

⁷   He raises the poor from the dust,
   lifts the needy from the rubbish heap,
⁸   in order to give him a place among princes,
   among the princes of his people.

⁹   He causes the childless woman
   to live at home happily as a mother of children.

Halleluyah!

114 ¹   When Isra'el came out of Egypt,
   the house of Ya'akov from a people of foreign speech,
²   Y'hudah became [God's] sanctuary,
   Isra'el his domain.

³   The sea saw this and fled;
   the Yarden turned back;
⁴   the mountains skipped like rams,
   the hills like young sheep.

⁵   Why is it, sea, that you flee?
   Why, Yarden, do you turn back?
⁶   Why, mountains, do you skip like rams;
   and you hills like young sheep?

⁷   Tremble, earth, at the presence of the Lord,
   at the presence of the God of Ya'akov,
⁸   who turned the rock into a pool of water,
   flint into flowing spring.

115 ¹   Not to us, *Adonai*, not to us,
   but to your name give glory,
   because of your grace and truth.

²   Why should the nations ask,
   "Where is their God?"
³   Our God is in heaven;
   he does whatever pleases him.

⁴ Their idols are mere silver and gold,
made by human hands.
⁵ They have mouths, but they can't speak;
they have eyes, but they can't see;
⁶ they have ears, but they can't hear;
they have noses, but they can't smell;
⁷ they have hands, but they can't feel;
they have feet, but they can't walk;
with their throats they can't make a sound.
⁸ The people who make them will become like them,
along with everyone who trusts in them.

⁹ Isra'el, trust in *Adonai*!
He is their help and shield.
¹⁰ House of Aharon, trust in *Adonai*!
He is their help and shield.
¹¹ You who fear *Adonai*, trust in *Adonai*!
He is their help and shield.
¹² *Adonai* has kept us in mind,
and he will bless.
He will bless the house of Isra'el;
he will bless the house of Aharon;
¹³ he will bless those who fear *Adonai*,
great and small alike.

¹⁴ May *Adonai* increase your numbers,
both yours and those of your children.
¹⁵ May you be blessed by *Adonai*,
the maker of heaven and earth.
¹⁶ Heaven belongs to *Adonai*,
but the earth he has given to humankind.

¹⁷ The dead can't praise *Adonai*,
not those who sink down into silence.
¹⁸ But we will bless *Adonai*
from now on and forever.

Halleluyah!

116¹ I love that *Adonai* heard
my voice when I prayed;
² because he turned his ear to me,
I will call on him as long as I live.

³ The cords of death were all around me,
Sh'ol's constrictions held me fast;

120

I was finding only distress and anguish.
⁴ But I called on the name of *Adonai*:
"Please, *Adonai*! Save me!"

⁵ *Adonai* is merciful and righteous;
yes, our God is compassionate.
⁶ *Adonai* preserves the thoughtless;
when I was brought low, he saved me.
⁷ My soul, return to your rest!
For *Adonai* has been generous toward you.
⁸ Yes, you have rescued me from death,
my eyes from tears and my feet from falling.
⁹ I will go on walking in the presence of *Adonai*
in the lands of the living.
¹⁰ I will keep on trusting even when I say,
"I am utterly miserable,"
¹¹ even when, in my panic, I declare,
"Everything human is deceptive."

¹² How can I repay *Adonai*
for all his generous dealings with me?
¹³ I will raise the cup of salvation
and call on the name of *Adonai*.
¹⁴ I will pay my vows to *Adonai*
in the presence of all his people.

¹⁵ From *Adonai*'s point of view,
the death of those faithful to him is costly.
¹⁶ Oh, *Adonai*! I am your slave;
I am your slave, the son of your slave-girl;
you have removed my fetters.
¹⁷ I will offer a sacrifice of thanks to you
and will call on the name of *Adonai*.
¹⁸ I will pay my vows to *Adonai*
in the presence of all his people,
¹⁹ in the courtyards of *Adonai*'s house,
there in your very heart, Yerushalayim.

Halleluyah!

117 ¹ Praise *Adonai*, all you nations!
Worship him, all you peoples!
² For his grace has overcome us,
and *Adonai*'s truth continues forever.

Halleluyah!

118 [1] Give thanks to *Adonai*; for he is good,
for his grace continues forever.
[2] Now let Isra'el say,
"His grace continues forever."
[3] Now let the house of Aharon say,
"His grace continues forever."
[4] Now let those who fear *Adonai* say,
"His grace continues forever."

[5] From my being hemmed in I called on *Yah*;
he answered and gave me more room.
[6] With *Adonai* on my side, I fear nothing —
what can human beings do to me?
[7] With *Adonai* on my side as my help,
I will look with triumph at those who hate me.

[8] It is better to take refuge in *Adonai*
than to trust in human beings;
[9] better to take refuge in *Adonai*
than to put one's trust in princes.

[10] The nations all surrounded me;
in the name of *Adonai* I cut them down.
[11] They surrounded me on every side
in the name of *Adonai* I cut them down.
[12] They surrounded me like bees
but were extinguished [as quickly] as a fire in thorns;
in the name of *Adonai* I cut them down.

[13] You pushed me hard to make me fall,
but *Adonai* helped me.
[14] *Yah* is my strength and my song,
and he has become my salvation.

[15] The sound of rejoicing and victory
is heard in the tents of the righteous:
"*Adonai*'s right hand struck powerfully!
[16] *Adonai*'s right hand is raised in triumph!
Adonai's right hand struck powerfully!"

[17] I will not die; no, I will live
and proclaim the great deeds of *Yah*!
[18] *Yah* disciplined me severely,
but did not hand me over to death.

[19] Open the gates of righteousness for me;
I will enter them and thank *Yah*.

20 This is the gate of ADONAI;
the righteous can enter it.
21 I am thanking you because you answered me;
you became my salvation.

22 The very rock that the builders rejected
has become the cornerstone!
23 This has come from ADONAI,
and in our eyes it is amazing.
24 This is the day ADONAI has made,
a day for us to rejoice and be glad.

25 Please, ADONAI! Save us!
Please, ADONAI! Rescue us!
26 Blessed is he who comes in the name of ADONAI.
We bless you from the house of ADONAI.

27 ADONAI is God, and he gives us light.
Join in the pilgrim festival with branches
all the way to the horns of the altar.

28 You are my God, and I thank you.
You are my God; I exalt you.
29 Give thanks to ADONAI; for he is good,
for his grace continues forever.

119

א (Alef)

1 How happy are those whose way of life is blameless,
who live by the *Torah* of ADONAI!
2 How happy are those who observe his instruction,
who seek him wholeheartedly!
3 They do nothing wrong
but live by his ways.
4 You laid down your precepts
for us to observe with care.
5 May my ways be steady
in observing your laws.
6 Then I will not be put to shame,
since I will have fixed my sight on all your *mitzvot*.
7 I thank you with a sincere heart
as I learn your righteous rulings.
8 I will observe your laws;
don't completely abandon me!

ב (*Bet*)

9   How can a young man keep his way pure?
     By guarding it according to your word.
10   I seek you with all my heart;
     don't let me stray from your *mitzvot*.
11   I treasure your word in my heart,
     so that I won't sin against you.
12   Blessed are you, A*DONAI*!
     Teach me your laws.
13   I proclaim with my mouth
     all the rulings you have spoken.
14   I rejoice in the way of your instruction
     more than in any kind of wealth.
15   I will meditate on your precepts
     and keep my eyes on your ways.
16   I will find my delight in your regulations.
     I will not forget your word.

ג (*Gimel*)

17   Deal generously with your servant;
     then I will live and observe your word.
18   Open my eyes, so that I will see
     wonders from your *Torah*.
19   Though I'm just a wanderer on the earth,
     don't hide your *mitzvot* from me.
20   I am continually consumed
     with longing for your rulings.
21   You rebuke the proud, the cursed,
     who stray from your *mitzvot*.
22   Remove scorn and contempt from me,
     because I observe your instruction.
23   Even when princes sit and plot against me,
     your servant meditates on your laws.
24   Also your instructions are my delight;
     they are my counselors.

ד (*Dalet*)

25   I lie prostrate in the dust;
     revive me, in keeping with your word.
26   I told you of my ways, and you answered me;
     teach me your laws.
27   Make me understand the way of your precepts,
     and I will meditate on your wonders.
28   I am melting away from anxiety and grief;
     renew my strength, in keeping with your word.

29   Keep deceitful ways far from me,
      and favor me with your *Torah*.
30   I choose the way of trust;
      I set your rulings [before me].
31   I cling to your instruction;
      A*DONAI*, don't let me be put to shame!
32   I will run the way of your *mitzvot*,
      for you have broadened my understanding.

ה (*Heh*)

33   Teach me, A*DONAI*, the way of your laws;
      keeping them will be its own reward for me.
34   Give me understanding; then I will keep your *Torah*;
      I will observe it with all my heart.
35   Guide me on the path of your *mitzvot*,
      for I take pleasure in it.
36   Bend my heart toward your instructions
      and not toward selfish gain.
37   Turn my eyes away from worthless things;
      with your ways, give me life.
38   Fulfill your promise, which you made to your servant,
      which you made to those who fear you.
39   Avert the disgrace which I dread,
      for your rulings are good.
40   See how I long for your precepts;
      in your righteousness, give me life!

ו (*Vav*)

41   May your grace come to me, A*DONAI*,
      your salvation, as you promised;
42   then I will have an answer for those who taunt me;
      for I trust in your word.
43   Don't take away completely my power to speak the truth;
      for I put my hope in your rulings;
44   and I will keep your *Torah* always,
      forever and ever.
45   I will go wherever I like,
      for I have sought your precepts.
46   I will speak of your instructions even to kings
      without being ashamed.
47   I will delight myself in your *mitzvot*,
      which I have loved.
48   I will lift my hands to your *mitzvot*, which I love;
      and I will meditate on your laws.

ז (*Zayin*)

⁴⁹ Remember your promise to your servant,
through which you have given me hope.
⁵⁰ In my distress my comfort is this:
that your promise gives me life.
⁵¹ Though the arrogant scorn me completely,
I have not turned away from your *Torah*.
⁵² ADONAI, I keep in mind your age-old rulings;
in them I take comfort.
⁵³ Fury seizes me when I think of the wicked,
because they abandon your *Torah*.
⁵⁴ Your laws have become my songs
wherever I make my home.
⁵⁵ I remember your name, ADONAI, at night;
and I observe your *Torah*.
⁵⁶ This [comfort] has come to me,
because I observe your precepts.

ח (*Het*)

⁵⁷ ADONAI, I say that my task
is to observe your words.
⁵⁸ I beg your favor with my whole heart;
show pity to me, in keeping with your promise.
⁵⁹ I thought about my ways
and turned my feet toward your instruction.
⁶⁰ I hurry, I don't delay,
to observe your *mitzvot*.
⁶¹ Even when the cords of the wicked close around me,
I don't forget your *Torah*.
⁶² At midnight I rise to give you thanks
because of your righteous rulings.
⁶³ I am a friend of all who fear you,
of those who observe your precepts.
⁶⁴ The earth, ADONAI, is full of your grace;
teach me your laws.

ט (*Tet*)

⁶⁵ You have treated your servant well,
ADONAI, in keeping with your word.
⁶⁶ Teach me good judgment and knowledge,
because I trust in your *mitzvot*.
⁶⁷ Before I was humbled, I used to go astray;
but now I observe your word.
⁶⁸ You are good, and you do good;
teach me your laws.

69 The arrogant are slandering me,
    but I will wholeheartedly keep your precepts.
70 Their hearts are as thick as fat,
    but I take delight in your *Torah*.
71 It is for my good that I have been humbled;
    it was so that I would learn your laws.
72 The *Torah* you have spoken means more to me
    than a fortune in gold and silver.

ʼ (*Yud*)

73 Your hands made and formed me;
    give me understanding, so I can learn your *mitzvot*.
74 Those who fear you rejoice at the sight of me,
    because I put my hope in your word.
75 I know, ADONAI, that your rulings are righteous,
    that even when you humble me you are faithful.
76 Let your grace comfort me,
    in keeping with your promise to your servant.
77 Show me pity, and I will live,
    for your *Torah* is my delight.
78 Let the proud be ashamed, because they wrong me with lies;
    as for me, I will meditate on your precepts.
79 Let those who fear you turn to me,
    along with those who know your instruction.
80 Let my heart be pure in your laws,
    so that I won't be put to shame.

כ (*Kaf*)

81 I am dying to know your salvation;
    my hope is in your word.
82 My eyes fail from watching for your promise;
    I ask, "When will you comfort me?"
83 For I have shriveled like a wineskin in a smoky room;
    still, I don't forget your laws.
84 How long can your servant stay alive?
    When will you bring judgment on my persecutors?
85 The arrogant have dug pits for me to fall in;
    this is not in keeping with your *Torah*!
86 All your *mitzvot* [show your] faithfulness;
    they are hounding me with lies; help me!
87 They have nearly ended my life on earth,
    but I have not abandoned your precepts.
88 In keeping with your grace, revive me;
    and I will observe your spoken instructions.

ל (*Lamed*)

89 Your word continues forever, A*DONAI*,
firmly fixed in heaven;
90 your faithfulness through all generations;
you established the earth, and it stands.
91 Yes, it stands today, in keeping with your rulings;
for all things are your servants.
92 If your *Torah* had not been my delight,
I would have perished in my distress.
93 I will never forget your precepts,
for with them you have made me alive.
94 I am yours; save me
because I seek your precepts.
95 The wicked hope to destroy me,
but I focus on your instruction.
96 I see the limits of all perfection,
but your *mitzvah* has no bounds.

מ (*Mem*)

97 How I love your *Torah*!
I meditate on it all day.
98 I am wiser than my foes,
because your *mitzvot* are mine forever.
99 I have more understanding than all my teachers,
because I meditate on your instruction.
100 I understand more than my elders,
because I keep your precepts.
101 I keep my feet from every evil way,
in order to observe your word.
102 I don't turn away from your rulings,
because you have instructed me.
103 How sweet to my tongue is your promise,
truly sweeter than honey in my mouth!
104 From your precepts I gain understanding;
this is why I hate every false way.

נ (*Nun*)

105 Your word is a lamp for my foot
and light on my path.
106 I have sworn an oath and confirmed it,
that I will observe your righteous rulings.
107 I am very much distressed;
A*DONAI*, give me life, in keeping with your word.
108 Please accept my mouth's voluntary offerings, A*DONAI*;
and teach me your rulings.

109 I am continually taking my life in my hands,
yet I haven't forgotten your *Torah*.
110 The wicked have set a trap for me,
yet I haven't strayed from your precepts.
111 I take your instruction as a permanent heritage,
because it is the joy of my heart.
112 I have resolved to obey your laws
forever, at every step.

ס (*Samekh*)

113 I hate doubleminded people,
but I love your *Torah*.
114 You are my hiding-place and shield;
I put my hope in your word.
115 Leave me alone, you evildoers,
so that I can keep my God's *mitzvot*.
116 Uphold me, as you promised; and I will live;
don't disappoint me in my hope.
117 Support me; and I will be saved,
always putting my attention on your laws.
118 You reject all who stray from your laws,
for what they deceive themselves with is false.
119 You discard the wicked of the earth like slag;
this is why I love your instruction.
120 My body trembles for fear of you;
your rulings make me afraid.

ע (*'Ayin*)

121 I have done what is just and right;
don't abandon me to my oppressors.
122 Guarantee your servant's well-being;
don't let the arrogant oppress me.
123 My eyes fail from watching for your salvation
and for [the fulfillment of] your righteous promise.
124 Deal with your servant in accordance with your grace,
and teach me your laws.
125 I am your servant; give me understanding,
so that I can know your instruction.
126 The time has come for *Adonai* to act,
because they are breaking your *Torah*.
127 Therefore I love your *mitzvot*
more than gold, more than fine gold.
128 Thus I direct my steps by [your] precepts;
every false way I hate.

פ (*Peh*)

129 Your instruction is a wonder;
    this is why I follow it.
130 Your words are a doorway that lets in light,
    giving understanding to the thoughtless.
131 My mouth is wide open, as I pant
    with longing for your *mitzvot*.
132 Turn to me, and show me your favor;
    in keeping with [your] judgment for those who love your name.
133 Guide my footsteps by your word;
    don't let any kind of sin rule me.
134 Redeem me from human oppression,
    and I will observe your precepts.
135 Make your face shine on your servant,
    and teach me your laws.
136 Rivers of tears flow down from my eyes,
    because they don't observe your *Torah*.

צ (*Tzadeh*)

137 You are righteous, ADONAI;
    and your rulings are upright.
138 You have commanded your instructions
    in righteousness and great faithfulness.
139 My zeal is destroying me,
    because my foes have forgotten your words.
140 Your word is refined to complete purity,
    and your servant loves it.
141 I may be small and despised,
    but I do not forget your precepts.
142 Your righteousness is eternal righteousness,
    and your *Torah* is truth.
143 Trouble and distress have overtaken me,
    but your *mitzvot* are my delight.
144 Your instruction is righteous forever;
    give me understanding, and I will live.

ק (*Kuf*)

145 Wholeheartedly I am calling on you;
    answer me, ADONAI; I will keep your laws.
146 I am calling on you; save me;
    and I will observe your instruction.
147 I rise before dawn and cry for help;
    I put my hope in your word.
148 My eyes are open before the night watches,
    so that I can meditate on your promise.

149 In your grace, hear my voice;
 ADONAI, in keeping with your justice, revive me.
150 The pursuers of carnality are getting close;
 they are distancing themselves from your *Torah*.
151 You are close by, ADONAI;
 and all your *mitzvot* are truth.
152 Long ago I learned from your instruction
 that you established it forever.

ר (*Resh*)

153 Look at my distress, and rescue me,
 for I do not forget your *Torah*.
154 Plead my cause, and redeem me;
 in keeping with your promise, revive me.
155 Salvation is far away from the wicked,
 because they don't seek your laws.
156 Great is your compassion, ADONAI;
 in keeping with your rulings, revive me.
157 Although my persecutors and foes are many,
 I have not turned away from your instruction.
158 I look at traitors with disgust,
 because they don't keep your word.
159 See how I love your precepts, ADONAI;
 in keeping with your grace, revive me.
160 The main thing about your word is that it's true;
 and all your just rulings last forever.

ש (*Shin*)

161 Princes persecute me for no reason,
 but my heart stands in awe of your words.
162 I take joy in your promise,
 like someone who finds much booty.
163 I hate falsehood, I detest it;
 but I love your *Torah*.
164 I praise you seven times a day
 because of your righteous rulings.
165 Those who love your *Torah* have great peace;
 nothing makes them stumble.
166 I hope for your deliverance, ADONAI;
 I obey your *mitzvot*.
167 My soul observes your instruction,
 and I love it so much!
168 I observe your precepts and instruction,
 for all my ways lie open before you.

ת (*Tav*)

169 Let my cry come before you, A*DONAI*;
in keeping with your word, give me understanding.
170 Let my prayer come before you;
in keeping with your promise, rescue me.
171 Let my lips speak praise,
because you teach me your laws.
172 Let my tongue sing of your promise,
because all your *mitzvot* are righteous.
173 Let your hand be ready to help me,
because I choose your precepts.
174 I long for your deliverance, A*DONAI*;
and your *Torah* is my delight.
175 Let me live, and I will praise you;
let your rulings help me.
176 I strayed like a lost sheep; seek out your servant;
for I do not forget your *mitzvot*.

120 ¹⁽⁰⁾ A song of ascents:

(1) I called to A*DONAI* in my distress,
and he answered me.
2 Rescue me, A*DONAI*, from lips that tell lies,
from a tongue full of deceit.

3 What has he in store for you, deceitful tongue?
What more will he do to you?
4 A warrior's sharp arrows,
with red-hot coals from a broom tree.

5 How wretched I am, that I'm an alien in Meshekh,
that I must live among the tents of Keidar!
6 I have had to live far too long
with those who hate peace.
7 I am all for peace;
but when I speak, they are for war.

121 ¹⁽⁰⁾ A song of ascents:

(1) If I raise my eyes to the hills,
from where will my help come?
2 My help comes from A*DONAI*,
the maker of heaven and earth.

³ He will not let your foot slip —
your guardian is not asleep.
⁴ No, the guardian of Isra'el
never slumbers or sleeps.

⁵ ADONAI is your guardian; at your right hand
ADONAI provides you with shade —
⁶ the sun can't strike you during the day
or even the moon at night.

⁷ ADONAI will guard you against all harm;
he will guard your life.
⁸ ADONAI will guard your coming and going
from now on and forever.

122 ¹⁽⁰⁾ A song of ascents. By David:

⁽¹⁾ I was glad when they said to me,
"The house of ADONAI! Let's go!"
² Our feet were already standing
at your gates, Yerushalayim.

³ Yerushalayim, built as a city
fostering friendship and unity.

⁴ The tribes have gone up there, the tribes of ADONAI,
as a witness to Isra'el,
to give thanks to the name of ADONAI.
⁵ For there the thrones of justice were set up,
the thrones of the house of David.

⁶ Pray for *shalom* in Yerushalayim;
may those who love you prosper.
⁷ May *shalom* be within your ramparts,
prosperity in your palaces.

⁸ For the sake of my family and friends, I say,
"*Shalom* be within you!"
⁹ For the sake of the house of ADONAI our God,
I will seek your well-being.

123 ¹⁽⁰⁾ A song of ascents:

⁽¹⁾ I raise my eyes to you,
whose throne is in heaven.

2   As a servant looks to the hand of his master,
     or a slave-girl to the hand of her mistress,
     so our eyes turn to ADONAI our God,
     until he has mercy on us.

3   Have mercy on us, ADONAI, have mercy;
     for we have had our fill of contempt,
4   more than our fill of scorn from the complacent
     and contempt from the arrogant.

124 ¹⁽⁰⁾ A song of ascents. By David:

(1)   If ADONAI hadn't been for us —
      let Isra'el repeat it —
2   If ADONAI hadn't been for us
      when people rose to attack us,
3   then, when their anger blazed against us,
      they would have swallowed us alive!
4   Then the water would have engulfed us,
      the torrent would have swept over us.
5   Yes, the raging water
      would have swept right over us.

6   Blessed be ADONAI, who did not leave us
      to be a prey for their teeth!
7   We escaped like a bird from the hunter's trap;
      the trap is broken, and we have escaped.

8   Our help is in the name of ADONAI,
      the maker of heaven and earth.

125 ¹⁽⁰⁾ A song of ascents:

(1)   Those who trust in ADONAI
      are like Mount Tziyon,
      which cannot be moved
      but remains forever.

2   Yerushalayim!
      Mountains all around it!
      Thus ADONAI is around his people
      henceforth and forever.

3   For the scepter of wickedness
      will not rule the inheritance of the righteous,

so that the righteous will not themselves
turn their hands to evil.
4   Do good, ADONAI, to the good,
to those upright in their hearts.
5   But as for those who turn aside
to their own crooked ways,
may ADONAI turn them away,
along with those who do evil.

Shalom on Isra'el!

126 ⁽⁰⁾ A song of ascents:

(1)   When ADONAI restored Tziyon's fortunes,
we thought we were dreaming.
2   Our mouths were full of laughter,
and our tongues shouted for joy.

Among the nations it was said,
"ADONAI has done great things for them!"
3   ADONAI did do great things with us;
and we are overjoyed.

4   Return our people from exile, ADONAI,
as streams fill *vadi*s in the Negev.

5   Those who sow in tears
will reap with cries of joy.
6   He who goes out weeping
as he carries his sack of seed
will come home with cries of joy
as he carries his sheaves of grain.

127 ⁽⁰⁾ A song of ascents. By Shlomo:

(1)   Unless ADONAI builds the house,
its builders work in vain.
Unless ADONAI guards the city,
the guard keeps watch in vain.

2   In vain do you get up early
and put off going to bed,
working hard to earn a living;
for he provides for his beloved,
even when they sleep.

3   Children too are a gift from *Adonai*;
      the fruit of the womb is a reward.
4   The children born when one is young
      are like arrows in the hand of a warrior.
5   How blessed is the man
      who has filled his quiver with them;
      he will not have to be embarrassed
      when contending with foes at the city gate.

128 ¹⁽⁰⁾ A song of ascents:

(1)   How happy is everyone who fears *Adonai*,
      who lives by his ways.

2   You will eat what your hands have produced;
      you will be happy and prosperous.
3   Your wife will be like a fruitful vine
      in the inner parts of your house.
      Your children around the table will be
      like shoots from an olive tree.

4   This is the kind of blessing that will fall
      on him who fears *Adonai*.

5   May *Adonai* bless you from Tziyon!
      May you see Yerushalayim prosper
      all the days of your life,
6   and may you live to see your children's children!

      Shalom on Isra'el.

129 ¹⁽⁰⁾ A song of ascents:

(1)   Since I was young they have often attacked me —
      let Isra'el repeat it —
2   since I was young they have often attacked me,
      but they haven't overcome me.

3   The plowmen plowed on my back;
      wounding me with long furrows.
4   But *Adonai* is righteous;
      he cuts me free from the yoke of the wicked.

5   Let all who hate Tziyon
      be thrown back in confusion.

6   Let them be like grass on the roof,
which dries out before it grows up
7   and never fills the reaper's hands
or the arms of the one who binds sheaves,
8   so that no passer-by says,
"Adonai's blessing on you!
We bless you in the name of Adonai!"

130 ¹⁽¹⁾ A song of ascents. By David:

(1)   Adonai, I call to you from the depths;
2   hear my cry, Adonai!
Let your ears pay attention
to the sound of my pleading.

3   Yah, if you kept a record of sins,
who, Adonai, could stand?
4   But with you there is forgiveness,
so that you will be feared.

5   I wait longingly for Adonai;
I put my hope in his word.
6   Everything in me waits for Adonai
more than guards on watch wait for morning,
more than guards on watch wait for morning.

7   Isra'el, put your hope in Adonai!
For grace is found with Adonai,
and with him is unlimited redemption.
8   He will redeem Isra'el
from all their wrongdoings.

131 ¹⁽¹⁾ A song of ascents. By David:

(1)   Adonai, my heart isn't proud;
I don't set my sight too high,
I don't take part in great affairs
or in wonders far beyond me.
2   No, I keep myself calm and quiet,
like a little child on its mother's lap —
I keep myself like a little child.

3   Isra'el, put your hope in Adonai
from now on and forever!

132 [1(0)] A song of ascents:

[(1)]   ADONAI, remember in David's favor
all the hardships he endured,
[2]   how he swore to ADONAI,
vowed to the Mighty One of Ya'akov,

[3]   "I will not enter the house where I live
or get into my bed,
[4]   I will not allow myself to sleep
or even close my eyes,
[5]   until I find a place for ADONAI,
a dwelling for the Mighty One of Ya'akov."

[6]   We heard about it in Efrat,
we found it in the Fields of Ya'ar.
[7]   Let's go into his dwelling
and prostrate ourselves at his footstool.

[8]   Go up, ADONAI, to your resting-place,
you and the ark through which you give strength.
[9]   May your *cohanim* be clothed with righteousness;
may those loyal to you shout for joy.
[10]   For the sake of your servant David,
don't turn away the face of your anointed one.

[11]   ADONAI swore an oath to David,
an oath he will not break:
"One of the sons from your own body
I will set on your throne.
[12]   If your sons keep my covenant
and my instruction, which I will teach them,
then their descendants too, forever,
will sit on your throne."

[13]   For ADONAI has chosen Tziyon,
he has wanted it as his home.
[14]   "This is my resting-place forever,
I will live here because I so much want to.
[15]   I will bless it with plenty of meat,
I will give its poor their fill of food.
[16]   Its *cohanim* I will clothe with salvation,
and its faithful will shout for joy.
[17]   I will make a king sprout there from David's line
and prepare a lamp for my anointed one.
[18]   His enemies I will clothe with shame,
but on him there will be a shining crown."

133 [1(0)] A song of ascents. By David:

(1)   Oh, how good, how pleasant it is
         for brothers to live together in harmony.

2   It is like fragrant oil on the head
         that runs down over the beard,
         over the beard of Aharon,
         and flows down on the collar of his robes.

3   It is like the dew of Hermon
         that settles on the mountains of Tziyon.
         For it was there that ADONAI ordained
         the blessing of everlasting life.

134 [1(0)] A song of ascents:

(1)   Come, bless ADONAI, all you servants of ADONAI,
         who serve each night in the house of ADONAI.
2   Lift your hands toward the sanctuary,
         and bless ADONAI.
3   May ADONAI, the maker of heaven and earth,
         bless you from Tziyon.

135 [1(0)] *Halleluyah!*

(1)   Give praise to the name of ADONAI!
         Servants of ADONAI, give praise!
2   You who stand in the house of ADONAI,
         in the courtyards of the house of our God,
3   praise *Yah*, for ADONAI is good;
         sing to his name, because it is pleasant.

4   For *Yah* chose Ya'akov for himself,
         Isra'el as his own unique treasure.
5   I know that ADONAI is great,
         that our Lord is above all gods.
6   ADONAI does whatever pleases him,
         in heaven, on earth, in the seas, in all the depths.
7   He raises clouds from the ends of the earth,
         he makes the lightning flash in the rain
         and brings the wind out from his storehouses.

8   He struck down Egypt's firstborn,
         humans and animals alike.

9   He sent signs and wonders among you, Egypt,
         against Pharaoh and all his subjects.
10   He struck many nations,
         and slaughtered mighty kings —
11   Sichon king of the Emori,
         'Og king of Bashan,
         and all the kingdoms of Kena'an.
12   Then he gave their land as a heritage,
         to be possessed by Isra'el his people.

13   *ADONAI*, your name continues forever,
         your renown, *ADONAI*, through all generations.
14   For *ADONAI* will vindicate his people,
         he will take pity on his servants.

15   The idols of the nations are mere silver and gold,
         made by human hands.
16   They have mouths, but they can't speak;
         they have eyes, but they can't see;
17   they have ears, but they can't listen;
         and they have no breath in their mouths.
18   The people who make them will become like them,
         along with everyone who trusts in them.

19   House of Isra'el, bless *ADONAI*!
         House of Aharon, bless *ADONAI*!
20   House of Levi, bless *ADONAI*!
         You who fear *ADONAI*, bless *ADONAI*!
21   Blessed be *ADONAI* out of Tziyon,
         he who dwells in Yerushalayim!

     Halleluyah!

136 1   Give thanks to *ADONAI*, for he is good,
         for his grace continues forever.
2   Give thanks to the God of gods,
         for his grace continues forever.
3   Give thanks to the Lord of lords,
         for his grace continues forever;

4   to him who alone has done great wonders,
         for his grace continues forever;
5   to him who skillfully made the heavens,
         for his grace continues forever;
6   to him who spread out the earth on the water,
         for his grace continues forever;

7   to him who made the great lights,
    for his grace continues forever;
8   the sun to rule the day,
    for his grace continues forever;
9   the moon and stars to rule the night,
    for his grace continues forever;

10 to him who struck down Egypt's firstborn,
    for his grace continues forever;
11 and brought Isra'el out from among them,
    for his grace continues forever;
12 with a mighty hand and an outstretched arm,
    for his grace continues forever;

13 to him who split apart the Sea of Suf,
    for his grace continues forever;
14 and made Isra'el cross right through it,
    for his grace continues forever;
15 but swept Pharaoh and his army into the Sea of Suf,
    for his grace continues forever;

16 to him who led his people through the desert,
    for his grace continues forever;
17 to him who struck down great kings,
    for his grace continues forever;
18 yes, he slaughtered powerful kings,
    for his grace continues forever;
19 Sichon king of the Emori,
    for his grace continues forever;
20 and 'Og king of Bashan,
    for his grace continues forever;

21 then he gave their land as a heritage,
    for his grace continues forever;
22 to be possessed by Isra'el his servant,
    for his grace continues forever;

23 who remembers us whenever we are brought low,
    for his grace continues forever;
24 and rescues us from our enemies,
    for his grace continues forever;

25 who provides food for every living creature,
    for his grace continues forever.

26 Give thanks to the God of heaven,
    for his grace continues forever.

137¹ By the rivers of Bavel we sat down and wept
as we remembered Tziyon.

² We had hung up our lyres
on the willows that were there,

³ when those who had taken us captive
asked us to sing them a song;
our tormentors demanded joy from us —
"Sing us one of the songs from Tziyon!"

⁴ How can we sing a song about A<small>DONAI</small>
here on foreign soil?

⁵ If I forget you, Yerushalayim,
may my right hand wither away!

⁶ May my tongue stick to the roof of my mouth
if I fail to remember you,
if I fail to count Yerushalayim
the greatest of all my joys.

⁷ Remember, A<small>DONAI</small>, against the people of Edom
the day of Yerushalayim's fall,
how they cried, "Tear it down! Tear it down!
Raze it to the ground!"

⁸ Daughter of Bavel, you will be destroyed!
A blessing on anyone who pays you back
for the way you treated us!

⁹ A blessing on anyone who seizes your babies
and smashes them against a rock!

138 ¹⁽⁰⁾ By David:

⁽¹⁾ I give you thanks with all my heart.
Not to idols, but to you I sing praise.

² I bow down toward your holy temple
and give thanks to your name for your grace and truth;
for you have made your word [even] greater
than the whole of your reputation.

³ When I called, you answered me,
you made me bold and strong.

⁴ All the kings of the earth will thank you, A<small>DONAI</small>,
when they hear the words you have spoken.

⁵ They will sing about A<small>DONAI</small>'s ways,
"Great is the glory of A<small>DONAI</small>!"

⁶ For though A<small>DONAI</small> is high, he cares for the lowly;
while the proud he perceives from afar.

⁷ You keep me alive when surrounded by danger;
you put out your hand when my enemies rage;

with your right hand you save me.
8   *Adonai* will fulfill his purpose for me.
Your grace, *Adonai*, continues forever.
Don't abandon the work of your hands!

139 ¹⁽¹⁾ For the leader. A psalm of David:

⁽¹⁾   *Adonai*, you have probed me, and you know me.
2   You know when I sit and when I stand up,
you discern my inclinations from afar,
3   you scrutinize my daily activities.
You are so familiar with all my ways
4   that before I speak even a word, *Adonai*,
you know all about it already.
5   You have hemmed me in both behind and in front
and laid your hand on me.
6   Such wonderful knowledge is beyond me,
far too high for me to reach.

7   Where can I go to escape your Spirit?
Where can I flee from your presence?
8   If I climb up to heaven, you are there;
if I lie down in Sh'ol, you are there.
9   If I fly away with the wings of the dawn
and land beyond the sea,
10   even there your hand would lead me,
your right hand would hold me fast.
11   If I say, "Let darkness surround me,
let the light around me be night,"
12   even darkness like this
is not too dark for you;
rather, night is as clear as day,
darkness and light are the same.

13   For you fashioned my inmost being,
you knit me together in my mother's womb.
14   I thank you because I am awesomely made,
wonderfully; your works are wonders —
I know this very well.
15   My bones were not hidden from you
when I was being made in secret,
intricately woven in the depths of the earth.
16   Your eyes could see me as an embryo,
but in your book all my days were already written;
my days had been shaped
before any of them existed.

17 God, how I prize your thoughts!
How many of them there are!
18 If I count them, there are more than grains of sand;
if I finish the count, I am still with you.

19 God, if only you would kill off the wicked!
Men of blood, get away from me!
20 They invoke your name for their crafty schemes;
yes, your enemies misuse it.
21 ADONAI, how I hate those who hate you!
I feel such disgust with those who defy you!
22 I hate them with unlimited hatred!
They have become my enemies too.

23 Examine me, God, and know my heart;
test me, and know my thoughts.
24 See if there is in me any hurtful way,
and lead me along the eternal way.

140 $^{1(0)}$ For the leader. A psalm of David:

2(1) Rescue me, ADONAI, from evil people,
protect me from violent people.
3(2) They plan evil things in their hearts —
they continually stir up bitter strife.
4(3) They have made their tongues as sharp as a snake's;
viper's venom is under their lips.   (*Selah*)

5(4) Keep me, ADONAI, from the hands of the wicked,
protect me from violent people
who are trying to trip me up.
6(5) The arrogant hide snares for me;
they spread nets by the side of the road,
hoping to trap me there.   (*Selah*)

7(6) I said to ADONAI, "You are my God;
listen, ADONAI, to my plea for mercy."
8(7) ADONAI, Adonai, my saving strength,
my helmet shielding my head in battle,
9(8) ADONAI, don't grant the wicked their wishes;
make their plot fail, so they won't grow proud.   (*Selah*)
10(9) May the heads of those who surround me
be engulfed in the evil they spoke of, themselves.
11(10) May burning coals rain down on them,
may they be flung into the fire,
flung into deep pits,
never to rise again.

¹²⁽¹¹⁾ Let slanderers find no place in the land;
       let the violent and evil be hunted relentlessly.

¹³⁽¹²⁾ I know that ADONAI gives justice to the poor
       and maintains the rights of the needy.
¹⁴⁽¹³⁾ The righteous will surely give thanks to your name;
       the upright will live in your presence.

141 ¹⁽⁰⁾ A psalm of David:

⁽¹⁾ ADONAI, I have called you; come to me quickly!
       Listen to my plea when I call to you.
² Let my prayer be like incense set before you,
       my uplifted hands like an evening sacrifice.

³ Set a guard, ADONAI, over my mouth;
       keep watch at the door of my lips.
⁴ Don't let my heart turn to anything evil
       or allow me to act wickedly
       with men who are evildoers;
       keep me from eating their delicacies.

⁵ Let the righteous strike me, let him correct me;
       it will be an act of love.
       Let my head not refuse such choice oil,
       for I will keep on praying about their wickedness.
⁶ When their rulers are thrown down from the cliff,
       [the wicked] will hear that my words were fitting.
⁷ As when one plows and breaks the ground into clods,
       our bones are strewn at the mouth of Sh'ol.

⁸ For my eyes, ADONAI, Adonai, are on you;
       in you I take refuge; don't pour out my life.
⁹ Keep me from the trap they have set for me,
       from the snares of evildoers.
¹⁰ Let the wicked fall into their own nets,
       while I pass by in safety.

142 ¹⁽⁰⁾ A *maskil* of David, when he was in the cave. A prayer:

²⁽¹⁾ With my voice I cry to ADONAI,
       with my voice I plead to ADONAI for mercy.
³⁽²⁾ Before him I pour out my complaint,
       before him I tell my trouble.
⁴⁽³⁾ When my spirit faints within me,
       you watch over my path.

By the road that I am walking
they have hidden a snare for me.

5(4)   Look to my right, and see
that no one recognizes me.
I have no way of escape;
nobody cares for me.

6(5)   I cried out to you, ADONAI;
I said, "You are my refuge,
my portion in the land of the living."

7(6)   Listen to my cry,
for I have been brought very low.

Rescue me from my persecutors,
for they are too strong for me.

8(7)   Lead me out of prison,
so that I can give thanks to your name;
in me the righteous will be crowning themselves,
because you will have treated me generously.

143 ¹⁽⁰⁾ A psalm of David:

(1)   ADONAI, hear my prayer;
listen to my pleas for mercy.
In your faithfulness, answer me,
and in your righteousness.

2   Don't bring your servant to trial,
since in your sight no one alive
would be considered righteous.

3   For an enemy is pursuing me;
he has crushed my life into the ground
and left me to live in darkness,
like those who have been long dead.

4   My spirit faints within me;
my heart is appalled within me.

5   I remember the days of old,
reflecting on all your deeds,
thinking about the work of your hands.

6   I spread out my hands to you,
I long for you like a thirsty land.   (*Selah*)

7   Answer me quickly, ADONAI,
because my spirit is fainting.
Don't hide your face from me,
or I'll be like those who drop down into a pit.

8   Make me hear of your love in the morning,
    because I rely on you.
    Make me know the way I should walk,
    because I entrust myself to you.
9   ADONAI, rescue me from my enemies;
    I have hidden myself with you.
10 Teach me to do your will,
    because you are my God.
    Let your good Spirit guide me
    on ground that is level.
11 For your name's sake, ADONAI, preserve my life;
    in your righteousness, bring me out of distress.
12 In your grace, cut off my enemies;
    destroy all those harassing me;
    because I am your servant.

144 ⁽⁰⁾ By David:

(1)   Blessed be ADONAI, my rock,
      who trains my hands for war
      and my fingers for battle.
2   He shows me grace; and he is my fortress,
      my stronghold, in whom I find shelter,
      my shield, in whom I take refuge,
      who subdues my people under me.

3   ADONAI, what are mere mortals,
      that you notice them at all;
      humans, that you think about them?
4   Man is like a puff of wind,
      his days like a fleeting shadow.

5   ADONAI, lower the heavens, and come down;
      touch the mountains, make them pour out smoke.
6   Shoot out lightning, and scatter them;
      send out your arrows, and rout them.
7   Reach out your hands from on high;
      rescue me; save me out of deep water,
      out of the power of strangers,
8   whose mouths speak worthless words
      and whose right hands swear false oaths.

9   God, I will sing a new song to you;
      sing praises to you with a ten-stringed harp.
10   You give kings their victories;
      you save your servant David from the cruel sword.

11   Rescue me, save me from the power of strangers,
      whose mouths speak worthless words
      and whose right hands swear false oaths.

12   Our sons in their youth will be
      like full-grown saplings,
      our daughters will be like sculptured pillars
      fit for the corner of a palace.
13   Our barns are full with crops of every kind;
      the sheep in our fields number thousands, tens of thousands.
14   our oxen are well-fed,
      our city walls have no breach,
      our people are not taken captive,
      and there are no cries of protest in our cities' open places.
15   How happy the people who live in such conditions!
      How happy the people whose God is ADONAI!

145 ¹⁽⁰⁾ Praise. By David:

(1)   I will praise you to the heights, my God, the king;
      I will bless your name forever and ever.
2   Every day I will bless you;
      I will praise your name forever and ever.
3   Great is ADONAI and greatly to be praised;
      his greatness is beyond all searching out.
4   Each generation will praise your works to the next
      and proclaim your mighty acts.
5   I will meditate on the glorious splendor
      of your majesty and on the story of your wonders.
6   People will speak of your awesome power,
      and I will tell of your great deeds.
7   They will gush forth the fame of your abounding goodness,
      and they will sing of your righteousness.
8   ADONAI is merciful and compassionate,
      slow to anger and great in grace.
9   ADONAI is good to all;
      his compassion rests on all his creatures.
10   All your creatures will thank you, ADONAI,
      and your faithful servants will bless you.
11   They will speak of the glory of your kingship,
      and they will tell about your might;
12   to let everyone know of your mighty acts
      and the glorious majesty of your kingship.
13   Your kingship is an everlasting kingship,
      your reign continues through all generations.
14   ADONAI supports all who fall
      and lifts up all who are bent over.

15 The eyes of all are looking to you;
   you give them their food at the right time.
16 You open your hand
   and satisfy the desire of every living thing.
17 ADONAI is righteous in all his ways,
   full of grace in all he does.
18 ADONAI is close to all who call on him,
   to all who sincerely call on him.
19 He fulfills the desire of those who fear him;
   he hears their cry and saves them.
20 ADONAI protects all who love him,
   but all the wicked he destroys.
21 My mouth will proclaim the praise of ADONAI;
   all people will bless his holy name forever and ever.

146 1 *Halleluyah!*

Praise ADONAI, my soul!
2 I will praise ADONAI as long as I live.
I will sing praise to my God all my life.

3 Don't put your trust in princes
   or in mortals, who cannot help.
4 When they breathe their last, they return to dust;
   on that very day all their plans are gone.

5 Happy is he whose help is Ya'akov's God,
   whose hope is in ADONAI his God.
6 He made heaven and earth,
   the sea and everything in them;
   he keeps faith forever.

7 He secures justice for the oppressed,
   he gives food to the hungry.
   ADONAI sets prisoners free,
8 ADONAI opens the eyes of the blind,
   ADONAI lifts up those who are bent over.
   ADONAI loves the righteous.
9 ADONAI watches over strangers,
   he sustains the fatherless and widows;
   but the way of the wicked he twists.

10 ADONAI will reign forever,
   your God, Tziyon, through all generations.

Halleluyah!

147 [1]   *Halleluyah!*

How good it is to sing praises to our God!
How sweet, how fitting to praise him!
[2]   *Adonai* is rebuilding Yerushalayim,
gathering the dispersed of Isra'el.
[3]   He heals the brokenhearted
and binds up their wounds.
[4]   He determines how many stars there are
and calls them all by name.

[5]   Our Lord is great, his power is vast,
his wisdom beyond all telling.
[6]   *Adonai* sustains the humble
but brings the wicked down to the ground.

[7]   Sing to *Adonai* with thanks,
sing praises on the lyre to our God.
[8]   He veils the sky with clouds;
he provides the earth with rain;
he makes grass grow on the hills;
[9]   he gives food to the animals,
even to the young ravens when they cry.

[10]   He takes no delight in the strength of a horse,
no pleasure in a runner's speed.
[11]   *Adonai* takes pleasure in those who fear him,
in those who wait for his grace.

[12]   Glorify *Adonai*, Yerushalayim!
Praise your God, Tziyon!
[13]   For he strengthens the bars of your gates,
he blesses your children within you,
[14]   he brings peace within your borders,
he gives you your fill of the finest wheat.

[15]   He sends his word out over the earth,
his command runs swiftly.
[16]   Thus he gives snow like wool,
scatters hoarfrost like ashes,
[17]   sends crystals of ice like crumbs of bread —
who can withstand such cold?
[18]   Then he sends his word out and melts them;
he makes the winds blow, and the water flows.

[19]   He reveals his words to Ya'akov,
his laws and rulings to Isra'el.

²⁰ He has not done this for other nations;
they do not know his rulings.

Halleluyah!

148 ¹ *Halleluyah!*

Praise Adonai from the heavens!
Praise him in the heights!
² Praise him, all his angels!
Praise him, all his armies!

³ Praise him, sun and moon!
Praise him, all shining stars!
⁴ Praise him, highest heaven,
and waters above the heavens!

⁵ Let them praise the name of Adonai;
for he commanded, and they were created.
⁶ He established them forever and ever;
he has given a law to which they must conform.

⁷ Praise Adonai from the earth,
sea monsters and watery depths,
⁸ fire and hail, snow and mist,
storm-winds that obey his word,
⁹ mountains and every hill,
fruit trees and all cedars,
¹⁰ wild animals and all livestock,
creeping reptiles, flying birds,
¹¹ kings of the earth and all peoples,
princes and all rulers on earth,
¹² young men and women alike,
old men and children.

¹³ Let them praise the name of Adonai,
for his name alone is exalted;
his glory is above both earth and heaven.

¹⁴ He has increased the power of his people,
granted praise to all his faithful,
to the descendants of Isra'el,
a people close to him.

Halleluyah!

149 ¹ *Halleluyah!*

Sing to A<small>DONAI</small> a new song,
his praise in the assembly of the faithful.
² Let Isra'el rejoice in their maker,
let Tziyon's children take joy in their king.
³ Let them praise his name with dancing,
make melody to him with tambourine and lyre;
⁴ for A<small>DONAI</small> takes delight in his people,
he crowns the humble with salvation.
⁵ Let the faithful exult gloriously,
let them sing for joy on their beds.

⁶ Let the high praises of God be in their throats,
but a two-edged sword in their hands
⁷ to carry out vengeance on the nations
and punishment on the peoples,
⁸ to bind their kings with chains
and put their nobles in irons,
⁹ to execute the judgments decreed for them;
for this will glorify all his faithful.

Halleluyah!

150 ¹ *Halleluyah!*

Praise God in his holy place!
Praise him in the heavenly dome of his power!
² Praise him for his mighty deeds!
Praise him for his surpassing greatness!

³ Praise him with a blast on the *shofar!*
Praise him with lute and lyre!
⁴ Praise him with tambourines and dancing!
Praise him with flutes and strings!
⁵ Praise him with clanging cymbals!
Praise him with loud crashing cymbals!
⁶ Let everything that has breath praise A<small>DONAI!</small>

Halleluyah!

"The fear of YHWH is the beginning of wisdom."

Proverbs Mishlei מִשְׁלֵי

Proverbs is packed with godly wisdom, presented in short pithy sayings, easy to understand and apply to your life. According to the *Jewish Encyclopedia* (1906), The Book of Proverbs contains "Wise, witty and pithy maxims or aphorisms from 1) Biblical collections, included in the canon; 2) Apocryphal collections, not included in the canon; 3) the Talmud; 4) collections of the Moorish-Spanish period; 5) miscellaneous works." The *Jewish Virtual Library* tells us that *Sefer Mishlei* [the Book of Proverbs], one of the three "wisdom books" of the Hagiographa [the Writings], represents the affirmative and didactic element in wisdom (*hokhmah*), in contrast to the radical questioning of Job and Ecclesiastes. In its present form the book appears to have served as a manual for the moral and religious instruction of the young. Comprising materials of various kinds gleaned from the long tradition of wisdom, the book was used in schools by professional sages (cf. Eccles. 12:9–12; Ecclus. 6:23–28). The teacher's objectives and methods are outlined in Proverbs 1:2–6, namely, cultivation of the mind and training in ethical principles by the use of proverbs (*mashal*), epigrams (*melizah*), sayings of the sages, and riddles (*hidah*) or puzzling questions. The teacher's basic theme is summed up in the motto with which he begins and ends the introduction to the older materials—"The fear of the Lord is the beginning [or first requirement, chief part] of knowledge [wisdom]" (1:7; 9:10). http://www.jewishvirtuallibrary.org/jsource/judaica/ejud_0002_0016_0_16139.html. *The Jewish Study Bible* (Oxford, 2004) states, "The English title of the book, Proverbs, is a misnomer, since the book contains more than proverbs. The Hebrew *mashal*, of which *mishlei*, proverbs, is a form of the plural, can also mean comparison" (p. 1447).

The authorship of Proverbs has long been a matter of dispute. Solomon's name appears in Proverbs 1:1, "The proverbs of Solomon the son of David, King of Israel," but there are also references within Proverbs to Agur (30:1) and Lemuel (31:1) as other authors. Solomon is often mentioned as someone who has extensive wisdom in the Bible as well as in extra-biblical literature. 1 Kings 4:32 (5:12 in Hebrew bibles) states that 3,000 proverbs and over 1,000 songs are said to have come from Solomon and it is also said that people came from all over the ancient world to hear the wisdom of Solomon.

The Book of Proverbs is referred to as wisdom literature along with several others: Ecclesiastes, the Song of Solomon, and certain Psalms, known as wisdom psalms. Throughout Proverbs, wisdom (or the wise person) is compared and contrasted with foolishness (or the fool). 'Fool' in Proverbs indicates one who is lacking in wisdom and uninterested in instruction, not one who is merely silly or playful. Wisdom is held up as something worth effort to attain and the reader is told that it starts with the person of YHWH: "The fear of YHWH is the beginning of wisdom."

In addition, throughout the instructions found in the various collections in Proverbs, wisdom is said in the discourse to come mostly from father to son (or mother to son in certain passages, for example, Lemuel, and parts of 1–9). This wisdom literature is concerned with the realities of human experience, from the mundane to the sublime, and with the relationship between that experience and the divine. Wisdom is personified throughout the text as a female figure who was the absolute first of God's creations and who existed before life inhabited the earth. When Wisdom speaks she speaks in the first person feminine and identifies herself, not just as the first companion of God, but also as the preserver of justice in civilization and the source of human advancement. Injustice by contrast is personified as a female adulteress luring unsuspecting male youths to their early death at the hands of a wrathful husband.

Three major themes of the collection of Proverbs have been suggested:

Family

In the society of ancient Israel, the family played an important role in the upbringing and education of children. Some internal evidence hints to the use of Proverbs in a family setting; the phrase "my son" appears some 20 times throughout the book. The role of the mother is also listed some 10 times.

Court

The name of Solomon stands in the title of the book, thus suggesting a royal setting. Throughout the Old Testament, wisdom is connected with the court.

School

It is possible that practical and reflective wisdom was transmitted in a house of learning or instruction.

The structure of Proverbs is as follows:
The Proverbs of Solomon (Proverbs 1–9)
Proverbial Sayings (Proverbs 10–22:16)
Thirty "Sayings of the Wise" (Proverbs 22:27 [17 in Hebrew bibles]–24:22)
Additional "Sayings of the Wise" (Proverbs 24:23–34)
Proverbs of Solomon copied by the men of Hezekiah (Proverbs 25–29)
Appendices (Proverbs 30–31)

Many of the truths in the Bible are like gold buried deep underground that take effort to dig out and understand. But the Book of Proverbs is like a mountain stream, littered with nuggets, just waiting to be picked up. Since there are 31 proverbs, you could choose one proverb a day and look for these nuggets that will enrich your life.

Mishlei
PROVERBS

1 ¹ The proverbs of Shlomo the son of David,
king of Isra'el,

² are for learning about wisdom and discipline;
for understanding words expressing deep insight;

³ for gaining an intelligently disciplined life,
doing what is right, just and fair;

⁴ for endowing with caution those who don't think
and the young person with knowledge and discretion.

⁵ Someone who is already wise
will hear and learn still more;
someone who already understands
will gain the ability to counsel well;

⁶ he will understand proverbs, obscure expressions,
the sayings and riddles of the wise.

⁷ The fear of *Adonai* is the beginning of knowledge,
but fools despise wisdom and discipline.

⁸ My son, heed the discipline of your father,
and do not abandon the teaching of your mother;

⁹ they will be a garland to grace your head,
a medal of honor for your neck.

¹⁰ My son, if sinners entice you,
don't go along with them.

¹¹ Suppose they say, "Come with us:
we'll ambush somebody and kill him,
we'll waylay some harmless soul, just for fun;

¹² we'll swallow him alive, like Sh'ol,
whole, like those who descend to the pit;

¹³ we'll find everything he has of value,
we'll fill our homes with loot!

¹⁴ Throw in your lot with us;
we'll share a common purse" —

¹⁵ my son, don't go along with them,
don't set foot on their path;

16   their feet run to evil,
        they rush to shed blood.
17   For in vain is the net baited
        if any bird can see it;
18   rather, they are ambushing themselves
        to shed their own blood, waylaying themselves.
19   So are the ways of all greedy for gain —
        it takes the lives of those who get it.

20   Wisdom calls aloud in the open air
        and raises her voice in the public places;
21   she calls out at streetcorners
        and speaks out at entrances to city gates:
22   "How long, you whose lives have no purpose,
        will you love thoughtless living?
        How long will scorners find pleasure in mocking?
        How long will fools hate knowledge?
23   Repent when I reprove —
        I will pour out my spirit to you,
        I will make my words known to you.
24   Because you refused when I called,
        and no one paid attention when I put out my hand,
25   but instead you neglected my counsel
        and would not accept my reproof;
26   I, in turn, will laugh at your distress,
        and mock when terror comes over you —
27   yes, when terror overtakes you like a storm
        and your disaster approaches like a whirlwind,
        when distress and trouble assail you.
28   Then they will call me, but I won't answer;
        they will seek me earnestly, but they won't find me.
29   Because they hated knowledge
        and did not choose the fear of ADONAI,
30   they refused my counsel
        and despised my reproof.
31   So they will bear the consequences of their own way
        and be overfilled with their own schemes.
32   For the aimless wandering of the thoughtless will kill them,
        and the smug overconfidence of fools will destroy them;
33   but those who pay attention to me will live securely,
        untroubled by fear of misfortune."

2 1   My son, if you will receive my words
        and store my commands inside you,
2   paying attention to wisdom
        inclining your mind toward understanding —

3   yes, if you will call for insight
and raise your voice for discernment,
4   if you seek it as you would silver
and search for it as for hidden treasure —
5   then you will understand the fear of A*DONAI*
and find knowledge of God.

6   For A*DONAI* gives wisdom;
from his mouth comes knowledge and understanding.
7   He stores up common sense for the upright,
is a shield to those whose conduct is blameless,
8   in order to guard the courses of justice
and preserve the way of those faithful to him.
9   Then you will understand righteousness, justice,
fairness and every good path.
10   For wisdom will enter your heart,
knowledge will be enjoyable for you,
11   discretion will watch over you,
and discernment will guard you.

12   They will save you from the way of evil
and from those who speak deceitfully,
13   who leave the paths of honesty
to walk the ways of darkness,
14   who delight in doing evil
and take joy in being stubbornly deceitful,
15   from those whose tracks are twisted
and whose paths are perverse.

16   They will save you from a woman who is a stranger,
from a loose woman with smooth talk,
17   who abandons the ruler she had in her youth
and forgets the covenant of her God.
18   Her house is sinking toward death,
her paths lead to the dead.
19   None who go to her return;
they never regain the path to life.
20   Thus you will walk on the way of good people
and keep to the paths of the righteous.
21   For the upright will live in the land,
the pure-hearted will remain there;
22   but the wicked will be cut off from the land,
the unfaithful rooted out of it.

3 1   My son, don't forget my teaching,
keep my commands in your heart;

2   for they will add to you many days,
     years of life and peace.

3   Do not let grace and truth leave you —
     bind them around your neck;
     write them on the tablet of your heart.
4   Then you will win favor and esteem
     in the sight of God and of people.

5   Trust in *Adonai* with all your heart;
     do not rely on your own understanding.
6   In all your ways acknowledge him;
     then he will level your paths.

7   Don't be conceited about your own wisdom;
     but fear *Adonai*, and turn from evil.
8   This will bring health to your body
     and give strength to your bones.

9   Honor *Adonai* with your wealth
     and with the firstfruits of all your income.
10   Then your granaries will be filled
     and your vats overflow with new wine.

11   My son, don't despise *Adonai*'s discipline
     or resent his reproof;
12   for *Adonai* corrects those he loves
     like a father who delights in his son.

13   Happy the person who finds wisdom,
     the person who acquires understanding;
14   for her profit exceeds that of silver,
     gaining her is better than gold,
15   she is more precious than pearls —
     nothing you want can compare with her.
16   Long life is in her right hand,
     riches and honor in her left.
17   Her ways are pleasant ways,
     and all her paths are peace.
18   She is a tree of life to those who grasp her;
     whoever holds fast to her will be made happy.

19   *Adonai* by wisdom founded the earth,
     by understanding he established the heavens,
20   by his knowledge the deep [springs] burst open
     and the dew condenses from the sky.

21 My son, don't let these slip from your sight;
   preserve common sense and discretion;
22 they will be life for your being
   and grace for your neck.
23 Then you will walk your way securely,
   without hurting your foot.
24 When you lie down, you will not be afraid;
   when you lie down, your sleep will be sweet.

25 Don't be afraid of sudden terror or destruction
   caused by the wicked, when it comes;
26 for you can rely on ADONAI;
   he will keep your foot from being caught in a trap.

27 Don't withhold good from someone entitled to it
   when you have in hand the power to do it.
28 Don't tell your neighbor, "Go away! Come another time;
   I'll give it to you tomorrow," when you have it now.
29 Don't plan harm against your neighbor
   who lives beside you trustingly.
30 Don't quarrel with someone for no reason,
   if he has done you no harm.
31 Don't envy a man of violence,
   don't choose any of his ways;
32 for the perverse is an abomination to ADONAI,
   but he shares his secret counsel with the upright.
33 ADONAI's curse is in the house of the wicked,
   but he blesses the home of the righteous.
34 The scornful he scorns,
   but gives grace to the humble.
35 The wise win honor,
   but fools win shame.

4 1 Listen, children, to a father's instruction;
   pay attention, in order to gain insight;
2 for I am giving you good advice;
   so don't abandon my teaching.
3 For I too was once a child to my father;
   and my mother, too, thought of me as her special darling.
4 He too taught me; he said to me,
   "Let your heart treasure my words;
   keep my commands, and live;
5 gain wisdom, gain insight;
   don't forget or turn from the words I am saying.
6 Don't abandon [wisdom]; then she will preserve you;
   love her, and she will protect you.

7 The beginning of wisdom is: get wisdom!
And along with all your getting, get insight!
8 Cherish her, and she will exalt you;
embrace her, and she will bring you honor;
9 she will give your head a garland of grace,
bestow on you a crown of glory."

10 Listen, my son, receive what I say,
and the years of your life will be many.
11 I'm directing you on the way of wisdom,
guiding you in paths of uprightness;
12 when you walk, your step won't be hindered;
and if you run, you won't stumble.
13 Hold fast to discipline, don't let it go;
guard it, for it is your life.

14 Don't follow the path of the wicked
or walk on the way of evildoers.
15 Avoid it, don't go on it,
turn away from it, and pass on.
16 For they can't sleep if they haven't done evil,
they are robbed of sleep unless they make someone fall.
17 For they eat the bread of wickedness
and drink the wine of violence.
18 But the path of the righteous is like the light of dawn,
shining ever brighter until full daylight.
19 The way of the wicked is like darkness;
they don't even know what makes them stumble.

20 My son, pay attention to what I am saying;
incline your ear to my words.
21 Don't let them out of your sight,
keep them deep in your heart;
22 for they are life to those who find them
and health to their whole being.

23 Above everything else, guard your heart;
for it is the source of life's consequences.
24 Keep crooked speech out of your mouth,
banish deceit from your lips.
25 Let your eyes look straight ahead,
fix your gaze on what lies in front of you.
26 Level the path for your feet,
let all your ways be properly prepared;
27 then deviate neither right nor left;
and keep your foot far from evil.

5 ^{1} My son, pay attention to my wisdom;
incline your ear to my understanding;
^{2} so that you will preserve discretion
and your lips keep watch over knowledge.

^{3} For the lips of a woman who is a stranger drop honey,
her mouth is smoother than oil;
^{4} but in the end she is as bitter as wormwood,
sharp as a double-edged sword.
^{5} Her feet go down to death,
her steps lead straight to Sh'ol;
^{6} she doesn't walk the level path of life —
her course wanders all over, but she doesn't know it.
^{7} So now, children, listen to me;
don't turn away from what I am saying:
^{8} distance your way from her,
stay far from the door of her house;
^{9} so that you won't give your vigor to others
and your years to someone who is cruel,
^{10} so strangers won't be filled with your strength
and what you worked for go to a foreign house.
^{11} Then, when your flesh and bones have shrunk,
at the end of your life, you would moan,
^{12} "How I hated discipline!
My whole being despised reproof,
^{13} I ignored what my teachers said,
I didn't listen to my instructors.
^{14} I took part in almost every kind of evil,
and the whole community knew it."

^{15} Drink the water from your own cistern,
fresh water from your own well.
^{16} Let what your springs produce be dispersed outside,
streams of water flowing in the streets;
^{17} but let them be for you alone
and not for strangers with you.
^{18} Let your fountain, the wife of your youth,
be blessed; find joy in her —
^{19} a lovely deer, a graceful fawn;
let her breasts satisfy you at all times,
always be infatuated with her love.
^{20} My son, why be infatuated with an unknown woman?
Why embrace the body of a loose woman?
^{21} For *Adonai* is watching a man's ways;
he surveys all his paths.
^{22} A wicked person's own crimes will trap him,
he will be held fast by the ropes of his sin.

23 He will die from lack of discipline;
    the magnitude of his folly will make him totter and fall.

6 ¹ My son, if you have put up security for your friend,
    if you committed yourself on behalf of another;
2   you have been snared by the words of your mouth,
    caught by the words of your own mouth.
3   Do this now, my son, and extricate yourself,
    since you put yourself in your friend's power:
    go, humble yourself, and pester your friend;
4   give your eyes no sleep,
    give your eyelids no rest;
5   break free, like a gazelle from the [hunter's] trap,
    like a bird from the grip of the fowler.

6   Go to the ant, you lazybones!
    Consider its ways, and be wise.
7   It has no chief, overseer or ruler;
8   yet it provides its food in summer
    and gathers its supplies at harvest-time.
9   Lazybones! How long will you lie there in bed?
    When will you get up from your sleep?
10 "I'll just lie here a bit, rest a little longer,
    just fold my hands for a little more sleep" —
11 and poverty comes marching in on you,
    scarcity hits you like an invading soldier.

12 A scoundrel, a vicious man,
    lives by crooked speech,
13 winking his eyes, shuffling his feet,
    pointing with his fingers.
14 With deceit in his heart,
    he is always plotting evil and sowing discord.
15 Therefore disaster suddenly overcomes him;
    unexpectedly, he is broken beyond repair.

16 There are six things ADONAI hates,
    seven which he detests:
17 a haughty look, a lying tongue,
    hands that shed innocent blood,
18 a heart that plots wicked schemes,
    feet swift in running to do evil,
19 a false witness who lies with every breath,
    and him who sows strife among brothers.

20 My son, obey your father's command,
    and don't abandon your mother's teaching.

21 Bind them always on your heart,
   tie them around your neck.
22 When you walk, they will lead you;
   when you lie down, they will watch over you;
   and when you wake up, they will talk with you.
23 For the *mitzvah* is a lamp, *Torah* is light,
   and reproofs that discipline are the way to life.

24 They keep you from an evil woman,
   from a loose woman's seductive tongue.
25 Don't let your heart lust after her beauty
   or allow her glance to captivate you.
26 The price of a whore is a loaf of bread,
   but the adulteress is hunting for a precious life.
27 Can a man carry fire inside his shirt
   without burning his clothes?
28 Can a man walk [barefoot] on hot coals
   without scorching his feet?
29 So is he who has sex with his neighbor's wife;
   anyone touching her will be punished.
30 A thief is not despised if he steals
   only to satisfy his appetite when hungry;
31 but even he, if caught, must pay back sevenfold;
   he may have to give up all the wealth that he owns.
32 He who commits adultery lacks sense;
   he who does it destroys himself.
33 He will get nothing but blows and contempt,
   and his disgrace will not be wiped away.
34 For jealousy drives a man into a rage;
   he will show no mercy when he takes revenge;
35 he will not accept compensation;
   he'll refuse every bribe, no matter how large.

7 1 My son, keep my words,
   store up my commands with you.
2 Obey my commands, and live;
   guard my teaching like the pupil of your eye.
3 Bind them on your fingers;
   write them on the tablet of your heart.
4 Say to wisdom, "You are my sister";
   call understanding your kinswoman;
5 so that they can keep you from unknown women,
   from loose women with their seductive talk.

6 For I was at the window of my house,
   glancing out through the lattice,

7   when I saw among the young men there,
        among those who don't think for themselves,
        a young fellow devoid of all sense.
8   He crosses the street near her corner
        and continues on toward her house.
9   Dusk turns into evening,
        and finally night, dark and black.
10   Then a woman approaches him,
        dressed as a prostitute, wily of heart.
11   She's the coarse, impulsive type,
        whose feet don't stay at home;
12   rather, she stalks the streets and squares,
        lurking at every streetcorner.

13   She grabs him, gives him a kiss,
        and, brazen-faced, she says to him,
14   "I had to offer peace sacrifices,
        and I fulfilled my vows today.
15   This is why I came out to meet you,
        to look for you; now I've found you.
16   I've spread quilts on my couch
        made of colored Egyptian linen.
17   I've perfumed my bed
        with myrrh, aloes and cinnamon.
18   Come on, let's make love till morning;
        we'll enjoy making love.
19   My husband isn't at home,
        he's gone on a long trip;
20   he took a bag of money with him
        and won't be back till the moon is full."

21   With all her sweet talk she convinces him,
        enticing him with her seductive words.
22   At once he follows her
        like an ox on its way to be slaughtered;
        like a fool to be punished in the stocks;
23   or like a bird rushing into a trap,
        not knowing its life is at stake
        till an arrow pierces its liver.

24   So now, children, listen to me;
        pay attention to what I am saying.
25   Don't let your heart turn to her ways;
        don't stray onto her paths.
26   For many are those she has struck down dead,
        numerous those she has killed.
27   Her house is the way to Sh'ol;
        it leads down to the halls of death.

8 [1]   Wisdom is calling!
        Understanding is raising her voice!
[2]   On the heights along the road,
        where the paths meet, she is standing;
[3]   by the gates leading into the city,
        at the entrances, she cries aloud:

[4]   "People, I am calling you,
        raising my voice to all mankind.
[5]   You who don't direct your lives,
        understand caution;
        as for you, you fools,
        get some common sense!

[6]   "Listen! I will say worthwhile things;
        when I speak, my words are right.
[7]   My mouth says what is true,
        because my lips detest evil.
[8]   All the words from my mouth are righteous;
        nothing false or crooked is in them.
[9]   They are all clear to those who understand
        and straightforward to those who gain knowledge.
[10]   Receive my instruction, rather than silver;
        knowledge, rather than the finest gold.
[11]   For wisdom is better than pearls;
        nothing you want can compare with her.

[12]   "I, wisdom, live together with caution;
        I attain knowledge and discretion.
[13]   The fear of ADONAI is hatred of evil.
        I hate pride and arrogance,
        evil ways and duplicitous speech.
[14]   Good advice is mine, and common sense;
        I am insight, power is mine.
[15]   By me kings reign,
        and princes make just laws.
[16]   By me princes govern,
        nobles too, and all the earth's rulers.
[17]   I love those who love me;
        and those who seek me will find me.
[18]   Riches and honor are with me,
        lasting wealth and righteousness.
[19]   My fruit is better than gold, fine gold,
        my produce better than the finest silver.
[20]   I follow the course of righteousness
        along the paths of justice,
[21]   to endow with wealth those who love me
        and fill their treasuries.

22 "ADONAI made me as the beginning of his way,
the first of his ancient works.
23 I was appointed before the world,
before the start, before the earth's beginnings.
24 When I was brought forth, there were no ocean depths,
no springs brimming with water.
25 I was brought forth before the hills,
before the mountains had settled in place;
26 he had not yet made the earth, the fields,
or even the earth's first grains of dust.
27 When he established the heavens, I was there.
When he drew the horizon's circle on the deep,
28 when he set the skies above in place,
when the fountains of the deep poured forth,
29 when he prescribed boundaries for the sea,
so that its water would not transgress his command,
when he marked out the foundations of the earth,
30 I was with him as someone he could trust.
For me, every day was pure delight,
as I played in his presence all the time,
31 playing everywhere on his earth,
and delighting to be with humankind.

32 "Therefore, children, listen to me:
happy are those who keep my ways.
33 Hear instruction, and grow wise;
do not refuse it.
34 How happy the person who listens to me,
who watches daily at my gates
and waits outside my doors.
35 For he who finds me finds life
and obtains the favor of ADONAI.
36 But he who misses me harms himself;
all who hate me love death."

9 1 Wisdom has built herself a house;
she has carved her seven pillars.
2 She has prepared her food, spiced her wine,
and she has set her table.
3 She has sent out her young girls [with invitations];
she calls from the heights of the city,
4 "Whoever is unsure of himself, turn in here!"
To someone weak-willed she says,
5 "Come and eat my food!
Drink the wine I have mixed!
6 Don't stay unsure of yourself, but live!
Walk in the way of understanding!"

7 "He who corrects a scoffer only gets insulted;
reproving a wicked man becomes his blemish.
8 If you reprove a scoffer, he will hate you;
if you reprove a wise man, he will love you.
9 Give to a wise man, and he grows still wiser;
teach a righteous man, and he will learn still more.
10 The fear of ADONAI is the beginning of wisdom,
and knowledge of holy ones is understanding.
11 For with me, your days will be increased;
years will be added to your life.
12 If you are wise, your wisdom helps you;
but if you scoff, you bear the consequences alone."

13 The foolish woman is coarse;
she doesn't think, and she doesn't know a thing.
14 She sits at the door of her house
or on a seat at the heights of the city,
15 calling to those who pass by,
to those going straight along their ways,
16 "Whoever is unsure of himself, turn in here!"
To someone weak-willed she says,
17 "Stolen water is sweet;
food eaten in secret is pleasant."
18 But he doesn't realize
that the dead are there,
and that those who accept her invitation
are in the depths of Sh'ol.

10 1 The proverbs of Shlomo:

A wise son is a joy to his father,
    but a foolish son is a grief to his mother.

2 No good comes from ill-gotten wealth,
    but righteousness rescues from death.
3 ADONAI does not let the righteous go hungry,
    but he thwarts the craving of the wicked.

4 Idle hands bring poverty;
    diligent hands bring wealth.
5 A sensible person gathers in summer,
    but he who sleeps during harvest is an embarrassment.

6 Blessings are for the head of the righteous,
    but the speech of the wicked is a cover for violence.
7 The memory of the righteous will be for a blessing,
    but the reputation of the wicked will rot.

8   Wise-hearted people take orders,
         but a babbling fool will have trouble.

9   He who walks purely walks securely,
         but he who walks in crooked ways will be found out.

10   He who winks his eye [instead of rebuking] causes pain,
         yet a babbling fool will have trouble.

11   The speech of the righteous is a fountain of life,
         but the speech of the wicked is a cover for violence.

12   Hate stirs up disputes,
         but love covers all kinds of transgressions.

13   On the lips of the intelligent is found wisdom,
         but a stick is in store for the back of a fool.
14   Wise people hide their knowledge,
         but when a fool speaks, ruin is imminent.

15   The wealth of the rich is his fortified city;
         the ruin of the poor is their poverty.

16   The activity of the righteous is for life;
         the income of the wicked is for sin.

17   He who observes discipline is on the way to life;
         but he who ignores correction is making a mistake.

18   He who covers up hate has lips that lie,
         and anyone who slanders is a fool.
19   When words are many, sin is not lacking;
         so he who controls his speech is wise.
20   The tongue of the righteous is like pure silver,
         but the mind of the wicked is worth little.
21   The lips of the righteous feed many,
         but fools die for lack of sense.

22   The blessing of Adonai is what makes people rich,
         and he doesn't mix sorrow with it.

23   To a fool, vileness is like a game,
         as is wisdom to a person of discernment.

24   What a fool dreads will overtake him,
         but the righteous will be given his desire.
25   When the storm has passed, the wicked are gone;
         but the righteous are firmly established forever.

²⁶ Like vinegar to the teeth and smoke to the eyes
is a lazy person to his employer.

²⁷ The fear of Adonai adds length to life,
but the years of the wicked are cut short.
²⁸ What the righteous hope for will end in joy;
what the wicked expect will come to nothing.
²⁹ The way of Adonai is a stronghold to the upright
but ruin to those who do evil.
³⁰ The righteous will never be moved,
but the wicked will not remain in the land.

³¹ The mouth of the righteous brings forth wisdom,
but the perverse tongue will be cut off.
³² The lips of the righteous know what is wanted,
but the mouth of the wicked [knows] deceit.

11 ¹ False scales are an abomination to Adonai,
but accurate weights please him.

² First comes pride, then disgrace;
but with the humble is wisdom.

³ The integrity of the upright guides them,
but the duplicity of the treacherous destroys them.

⁴ On the day of wrath, wealth doesn't help;
but righteousness rescues from death.

⁵ The righteousness of the innocent levels their way,
but the wickedness of the wicked makes them fall.
⁶ The righteousness of the upright rescues them,
but the treacherous are trapped by their own intrigues.
⁷ When a wicked man dies, his hope perishes;
what he hopes for from evil comes to nothing.
⁸ The righteous is delivered from trouble,
and the wicked comes to take his place.
⁹ With his mouth the hypocrite can ruin his neighbor,
but by knowledge the righteous are delivered.
¹⁰ When the righteous prosper, the city rejoices;
and when the wicked perish, there is joy.
¹¹ By the blessing of the upright, a city is raised up;
but the words of the wicked tear it down.

¹² He who belittles another lacks good sense,
whereas a person of discernment stays silent.

13   A gossip goes around revealing secrets,
        but a trustworthy person keeps a confidence.

14   Without clever tactics an army is defeated,
        and victory comes from much planning.

15   He who guarantees a loan for a stranger will suffer,
        but refusing to underwrite is safe.

16   A gracious woman obtains honor;
        aggressive men obtain wealth.

17   A man who is kind does himself good,
        but the cruel does harm to himself.

18   The profits of the wicked are illusory;
        but those who sow righteousness gain a true reward.
19   Genuine righteousness leads to life,
        but the pursuer of evil goes to his own death.
20   The crooked-hearted are an abomination to ADONAI,
        but those sincere in their ways are his delight.
21   Depend on it: the evil will not go unpunished;
        but the offspring of the righteous will escape.

22   Like a gold ring in the snout of a pig
        is a beautiful woman who lacks good sense.

23   The righteous desire only good,
        but what the wicked hope for brings wrath.

24   Some give freely and still get richer,
        while others are stingy but grow still poorer.
25   The person who blesses others will prosper;
        he who satisfies others will be satisfied himself.
26   The people will curse him who withholds grain;
        but if he sells it, blessings will be on his head.

27   He who strives for good obtains favor,
        but he who searches for evil — it comes to him!

28   He who trusts in his riches will fall,
        but the righteous will flourish like sprouting leaves.

29   Those who trouble their families inherit the wind,
        and the fool becomes slave to the wise.

30   The fruit of the righteous is a tree of life,
        and he who is wise wins souls.

³¹ If the righteous are paid what they deserve here on earth,
how much more the wicked and the sinner!

12¹ He who loves knowledge loves discipline,
but he who hates correction is a boor.

² A good man obtains ADONAI's favor,
but the schemer his condemnation.

³ No one is made secure by wickedness,
but the roots of the righteous will never be moved.

⁴ A capable wife is a crown for her husband,
but a shameful one is like rot in his bones.

⁵ The plans of the righteous are just,
but the schemes of the wicked are deceitful.
⁶ The words of the wicked are a deadly ambush,
but the speech of the upright rescues them.
⁷ Once the wicked are down, it's the end of them;
but the house of the upright endures.

⁸ A person wins praise in keeping with his common sense,
but a person with a warped mind is treated with contempt.

⁹ Better to be despised and have a servant
than to boast of one's status but have nothing to eat.

¹⁰ A righteous man takes care of his animal,
but the wicked? Even his compassion is cruel.

¹¹ He who farms his land will have plenty of food,
but he who follows futilities has no sense.

¹² The wicked covet the loot of evil men,
but the root of the righteous gives forth of itself.
¹³ The wicked is trapped by his own sinful speech,
but the righteous finds a way out of trouble.

¹⁴ One can be filled with good as the result of one's words,
and one gets the reward one's deeds deserve.

¹⁵ Fools suppose their way is straight,
but the wise pay attention to advice.
¹⁶ A fool's anger is known at once,
but a cautious person slighted conceals his feelings.

17 He who tells the truth furthers justice,
  but a false witness furthers deceit.

18 Idle talk can pierce like a sword,
  but the tongue of the wise can heal.
19 Truthful words will stand forever,
  lying speech but a moment.

20 Deceit is in the hearts of those who plot evil,
  but for those advising peace there is joy.
21 No harm can come to the righteous,
  but the wicked are overwhelmed with disaster.

22 Lying lips are an abomination to ADONAI,
  but those who deal faithfully are his delight.
23 A cautious person conceals knowledge,
  but the heart of a fool blurts out folly.

24 The diligent will rule,
  while the lazy will be put to forced labor.

25 Anxiety in a person's heart weighs him down,
  but a kind word cheers him up.

26 The righteous guides his friend's way rightly,
  but the way of the wicked will lead them astray.

27 A lazy man doesn't roast what he hunted;
  but when a man is diligent, his wealth is precious.

28 In the road of righteousness is life;
  no death is in its pathway.

13 1 A son who heeds his father's discipline is wise,
  but a scoffer doesn't listen to rebuke.

2 A [good] man enjoys good as a result of what he says,
  but the essence of the treacherous is violence.

3 He who guards his mouth preserves his life,
  but one who talks too much comes to ruin.

4 The lazy person wants but doesn't have;
  the diligent get their desires filled.

5 A righteous person hates lying,
  but the wicked is vile and disgraceful.

6   Righteousness protects him whose way is honest,
         but wickedness brings down the sinner.

7   There are those with nothing who pretend they are rich,
         also those with great wealth who pretend they are poor.
8   The rich man may have to ransom his life,
         but a poor man gets no threats.

9   The light of the righteous [shines] joyfully,
         but the lamp of the wicked will be extinguished.

10   Insolence produces only strife,
         but wisdom is found with those who take advice.

11   Wealth gotten by worthless means dwindles away,
         but he who amasses it by hard work will increase it.

12   Hope deferred makes the heart sick,
         but desire fulfilled is a tree of life.

13   He who despises a word will suffer for it,
         but he who respects a command will be rewarded.

14   The teaching of a wise man is a fountain of life,
         enabling one to avoid deadly traps.

15   Good common sense produces grace,
         but the way of the treacherous is rough.

16   Every cautious person acts with knowledge,
         but a fool parades his folly.

17   A wicked messenger falls into evil,
         but a faithful envoy brings healing.

18   Poverty and shame are for him who won't be taught,
         but he who heeds reproof will be honored.

19   Desire fulfilled is sweet to the soul,
         but turning away from evil is abhorrent to fools.
20   He who walks with the wise will become wise,
         but the companion of fools will suffer.

21   Evil pursues sinners,
         but prosperity will reward the righteous.
22   A good man leaves an inheritance to his grandchildren,
         but the wealth of a sinner is stored up for the righteous.

23   The fields of the poor may yield much food,
          but some are swept away because of injustice.

24   He who fails to use a stick hates his son,
          but he who loves him is careful to discipline him.

25   The righteous person eats his fill,
          but the belly of the wicked is empty.

14 ¹ Every wise woman builds up her home,
          but a foolish one tears it down with her own hands.

2   A person with upright conduct fears A*DONAI*,
          but a person who is devious scorns him.

3   From the mouth of a fool sprouts pride,
          but the lips of the wise protect them.

4   Where there are no oxen, the stalls are clean;
          but much is produced by the strength of an ox.

5   An honest witness will not lie,
          but a false witness lies with every breath.

6   A scoffer seeks wisdom in vain,
          but knowledge comes easily to someone with discernment.

7   Keep clear of a fool,
          for you won't hear a sensible word from him.
8   The wisdom of the cautious makes him know where he is going,
          but the folly of fools misleads them.
9   Guilt offerings make a mockery of fools;
          but among the upright there is good will.

10   The heart knows its own bitterness,
          and no stranger can share its joy.

11   The house of the wicked will be destroyed,
          but the tent of the upright will flourish.

12   There can be a way which seems right to a person,
          but at its end are the ways of death.

13   Even in laughter the heart can be sad,
          and joy may end in sorrow.

14 A backslider is filled up with his own ways,
    but a good person gets satisfaction from himself.

15 One who doesn't think believes every word,
    but the cautious understands his steps.

16 A wise person fears and turns away from evil,
    but a fool is reckless and overconfident.

17 He who is quick-tempered does stupid things,
    and one who does vile things is hated.

18 Thoughtless people inherit folly,
    but the cautious are crowned with knowledge.

19 The evil bow down before the good,
    and the wicked at the gates of the righteous.

20 The poor are disliked even by their peers,
    but the rich have many friends.

21 He who despises his fellow sins,
    but he who shows compassion to the humble is happy.

22 Won't those who plot evil go astray?
    But grace and truth are for those who plan good.

23 In all work there is profit,
    but mere talk produces only poverty.
24 The crown of the wise is their riches,
    but the folly of fools is just that — folly.

25 A truthful witness saves lives,
    but a liar misdirects [judgment].

26 In the fear of ADONAI is powerful security;
    for his children there will be a place of refuge.
27 The fear of ADONAI is a fountain of life
    enabling one to avoid deadly traps.

28 A king's glory lies in having many subjects;
    if the prince's people are few, it is his ruin.

29 Being slow to anger goes with great understanding,
    being quick-tempered makes folly still worse.

30 A tranquil mind gives health to the body,
    but envy rots the bones.

³¹   The oppressor of the poor insults his maker,
        but he who is kind to the needy honors him.

³²   The wicked are brought down by their wrongdoing,
        but the righteous can be confident even at death.

³³   Wisdom is at rest in a person with discernment,
        but in fools it has to call attention to itself.

³⁴   Righteousness makes a nation great,
        but sin degrades any people.

³⁵   A king shows favor to a servant with good sense,
        but his wrath strikes one who shames [him].

15¹   A gentle response deflects fury,
        but a harsh word makes tempers rise.
²   The tongue of the wise presents knowledge well,
        but the mouth of a fool spews out folly.

³   The eyes of ADONAI are everywhere,
        watching the evil and the good.

⁴   A soothing tongue is a tree of life,
        but when it twists things, it breaks the spirit.

⁵   A fool despises his father's discipline,
        but he who heeds warnings is prudent.

⁶   The home of the righteous is a storehouse of treasure,
        but the earnings of the wicked bring trouble.

⁷   The lips of the wise spread knowledge;
        not so the hearts of fools.

⁸   ADONAI detests the sacrifices of the wicked
        but delights in the prayers of the upright.
⁹   ADONAI detests the way of the wicked
        but loves anyone who pursues righteousness.

¹⁰   Discipline is severe for one who leaves the way,
        and whoever can't stand correction will die.

¹¹   Sh'ol and Abaddon lie open to ADONAI;
        so how much more people's hearts!

12 A scorner does not like being corrected;
       he won't go to the wise [for advice].

13 A glad heart makes a face happy,
       but heartache breaks the spirit.

14 The mind of a person with discernment seeks knowledge,
       but the mouth of a fool feeds on folly.

15 For the poor, every day is hard;
       but the good-hearted have a perpetual feast.

16 Better little with the fear of *ADONAI*
       than great wealth coupled with worry.

17 Better a vegetable dinner with love
       than a stall-fattened ox with hate.

18 Hot-tempered people stir up strife,
       but patient people quiet quarrels.

19 The lazy person's way seems overgrown by thorns,
       but the path of the upright is a level highway.

20 A wise son is a joy to his father,
       and only a fool despises his mother.

21 Folly appeals to one who lacks sense,
       but a person of discernment goes straight ahead.

22 Without deliberation, plans go wrong;
       but with many advisers, they succeed.

23 People take pleasure in anything they say;
       but a word at the right time, how good it is!

24 For the prudent, the path of life goes upward;
       thus he avoids Sh'ol below.

25 *ADONAI* will pull down the houses of the proud,
       but preserves intact the widow's boundaries.

26 *ADONAI* detests plans to do evil,
       but kind words are pure.

27 The greedy for gain brings trouble to his home,
       but he who hates bribes will live.

28 The mind of the righteous thinks before speaking,
       but the mouth of the wicked spews out evil stuff.

29   *Adonai* is far from the wicked,
         but he listens to the prayer of the righteous.

30   A cheerful glance brings joy to the heart,
         and good news invigorates the bones.

31   He who heeds life-giving correction
         will be at home in the company of the wise.
32   He who spurns discipline detests himself,
         but he who listens to correction grows in understanding.
33   The discipline of wisdom is fear of *Adonai*,
         so before being honored, a person must be humble.

16 1   A person is responsible to prepare his heart,
         but how the tongue speaks is from *Adonai*.

2   All a man's ways are pure in his own view,
         but *Adonai* weighs the spirit.

3   If you entrust all you do to *Adonai*,
         your plans will achieve success.

4   *Adonai* made everything for its purpose,
         even the wicked for the day of disaster.

5   *Adonai* detests all those with proud hearts;
         be assured that they will not go unpunished.

6   Grace and truth atone for iniquity,
         and people turn from evil through fear of *Adonai*.

7   When a man's ways please *Adonai*,
         he makes even the man's enemies be at peace with him.

8   Better a little with righteousness
         than a huge income with injustice.

9   A person may plan his path,
         but *Adonai* directs his steps.

10   Divine inspiration is on the lips of the king,
         so his mouth must be faithful when he judges.
11   The balance and scales of justice have their origin in *Adonai*;
         all the weights in the bag are his doing.
12   It is an abomination for a king to do evil,
         for the throne is made secure by righteousness.

13 The king should delight in righteous lips,
   and he should love someone who speaks what is right.
14 The king's anger is a herald of death,
   and one who is wise will appease it.
15 When the king's face brightens, it means life;
   his favor is like the clouds that bring spring rain.

16 How much better than gold it is to gain wisdom!
   Yes, rather than money, choose to gain understanding.

17 Avoiding evil is the highway of the upright;
   he who watches his step preserves his life.

18 Pride goes before destruction,
   and arrogance before failure.

19 Better to be humble among the poor
   than share the spoil with the proud.

20 He who has skill in a matter will succeed;
   he who trusts in ADONAI will be happy.

21 A wise-hearted person is said to have discernment,
   and sweetness of speech adds to learning.

22 Common sense is a fountain of life to one who has it,
   whereas fools are punished by their own folly.

23 The wise man's heart teaches his mouth,
   and to his lips it adds learning.
24 Pleasant words are like a honeycomb,
   sweet to the taste and healing for the body.

25 There can be a way which seems right to a person,
   but at its end are the ways of death.

26 A working man's appetite acts on his behalf,
   because his hunger presses him on.

27 A worthless person digs up evil [gossip] —
   it is like scorching fire on his lips.
28 A deceitful person stirs up strife,
   and a slanderer can separate even close friends.

29 A violent man lures his neighbor astray
   and leads him into evil ways.

30 One who winks knowingly is planning deceit;
   one who pinches his lips together has already done wrong.

31 White hair is a crown of honor
   obtained by righteous living.

32 He who controls his temper is better than a war hero,
   he who rules his spirit better than he who captures a city.

33 One can cast lots into one's lap,
   but the decision comes from ADONAI.

17 1 Better a dry piece of bread with calm
   than a house full of food but also full of strife.

2 An intelligent slave will rule a shameful son
   and share the inheritance with the brothers.

3 The crucible [tests] silver, and the furnace [tests] gold,
   but the one who tests hearts is ADONAI.

4 An evildoer heeds wicked lips;
   a liar listens to destructive talk.

5 He who mocks the poor insults his maker;
   he who rejoices at calamity will not go unpunished.

6 Grandchildren are the crown of the aged,
   while the glory of children is their ancestors.

7 Fine speech is unbecoming to a boor,
   and even less lying lips to a leader.

8 A bribe works like a charm, in the view of him who gives it —
   wherever it turns, it succeeds.

9 He who conceals an offense promotes love,
   but he who harps on it can separate even close friends.

10 A rebuke makes more impression on a person of understanding
   than a hundred blows on a fool.

11 An evil person seeks only rebellion,
   but a cruel messenger will be sent against him.

12 Rather meet a bear robbed of its cubs
   than encounter a fool in his folly.

13   Evil will not depart from the house
         of him who returns evil for good.

14   Starting a fight is like letting water through [a dike] ——
         better stop the quarrel before it gets worse.

15   He who justifies the wicked and he who condemns the righteous —
         both alike are an abomination to ADONAI.

16   Why would a fool wish to pay for wisdom
         when he has no desire to learn?

17   A friend shows his friendship at all times ——
         it is for adversity that [such] a brother is born.

18   He who gives his hand to guarantee a loan
         for his neighbor lacks good sense.

19   Those who love quarreling love giving offense;
         those who make their gates tall are courting disaster.

20   A crooked-hearted person will find nothing good,
         and the perverse of speech will end in calamity.

21   He who fathers a fool does so to his sorrow,
         and the father of a boor has no joy.

22   A happy heart is good medicine,
         but low spirits sap one's strength.

23   From under a cloak a bad man takes a bribe
         to pervert the course of justice.

24   The discerning person focuses on wisdom there before him,
         but a fool's eyes wander to the ends of the earth.

25   A son who is a fool means anger for his father
         and bitterness for the mother who gave him birth.

26   To punish the innocent is not right,
         likewise to flog noble people for their uprightness.

27   A knowledgeable person controls his tongue;
         a discerning person controls his temper.

28   Even a fool, if he stays silent, is thought wise;
         he who keeps his mouth shut can pass for smart.

18 [1]   He who separates himself indulges his desires
      and shows contempt for sound advice of any kind.

[2]   A fool takes no pleasure in trying to understand;
      he only wants to express his own opinion.

[3]   When a wicked person comes, contempt comes too,
      and with disdain, provocation.

[4]   The words of a man's mouth are deep water,
      a gushing torrent, a fountain of wisdom.

[5]   It is not good to be partial to the guilty
      and thus deprive the innocent of justice.

[6]   A fool's words get him into fights;
      yes, his mouth calls out for a beating.
[7]   A fool's mouth is his ruin;
      his words are a trap for him.
[8]   A slanderer's words are tasty morsels;
      they slide right down into the belly.

[9]   Whoever is lazy in doing his work
      is brother to the destroyer.

[10]   The name of *Adonai* is a strong tower;
      a righteous person runs to it and is raised high [above danger].
[11]   The wealth of the rich is his fortified city,
      like a high wall, in his own imagination.

[12]   Before being ruined, a person's heart is proud;
      before being honored, a person must be humble.

[13]   To answer someone before hearing him out
      is both stupid and embarrassing.

[14]   A person's spirit can sustain him when ill,
      but a crushed spirit — who can bear it?

[15]   The mind of a person with discernment gets knowledge,
      and the ear of the wise seeks knowledge.

[16]   A person's gift clears his way
      and gives him access to the great.

[17]   The first to state his case seems right,
      till the other one comes and cross-examines.

18   Casting lots puts an end to strife
        and separates powerful disputants.

19   It is harder to win an offended brother than a strong city;
        their fights are like the bars of a fortress.

20   A person's belly will be filled with the fruit of his mouth;
        with what his lips produce he will be filled.
21   The tongue has power over life and death;
        those who indulge it must eat its fruit.

22   He who finds a wife finds a great good;
        he has won the favor of Adonai.

23   The poor man speaks beseechingly,
        the rich man's answer is blunt.

24   Some "friends" pretend to be friends,
        but a true friend sticks closer than a brother.

19 1   Better to be poor and live one's life uprightly
        than engage in crooked speech, for such a one is a fool.

2   To act without knowing how you function is not good;
        and if you rush ahead, you will miss your goal.

3   A person's own folly is what ruins his way,
        but he rages in his heart against Adonai.

4   Wealth brings in many friends,
        but the poor man loses the one friend he has.

5   A false witness will not go unpunished;
        whoever breathes out lies will not escape.

6   Many ask favors of a generous person —
        to a giver of gifts, everyone is a friend.

7   A poor man's relatives all hate him;
        even more his friends stay away from him.
    He may pursue them with entreaties,
        but they aren't there to be found.

8   To acquire good sense is to love oneself;
        to treasure discernment is to prosper.

9   A false witness will not go unpunished;
        whoever breathes out lies will perish.

10   It isn't fitting for a fool to live in luxury,
        and even less for a slave to govern princes.

11   People with good sense are slow to anger,
        and it is their glory to overlook an offense.

12   A king's wrath is like the roaring of a lion,
        but his favor is like dew on the grass.

13   A son who is a fool is his father's ruin,
        and a nagging wife is like a leak that keeps dripping.
14   A house and wealth are inherited from ancestors,
        but a sensible wife is from ADONAI.

15   Laziness makes people fall asleep,
        and an idle person will go hungry.

16   He who keeps a *mitzvah* keeps himself safe,
        but he who doesn't care how he lives will die.

17   He who is kind to the poor is lending to ADONAI;
        and he will repay him for his good deed.

18   Discipline your child while there is hope,
        but don't get so angry that you kill him!

19   A violent-tempered person will be punished;
        if you try to save him from it, you make things worse.

20   Listen to advice, and accept discipline,
        so that in the end you will be wise.

21   One can devise many plans in one's mind,
        but ADONAI's plan will prevail.

22   A man's lust is his shame,
        and a poor man is better than a liar.

23   The fear of ADONAI leads to life;
        one who has it is satisfied and rests untouched by evil.

24   The lazy person buries his hand in the dish
        but doesn't even bother to bring it to his mouth.

25   If you strike a scorner,
>   the simple will learn to act wisely;
> if you reprove the intelligent,
>   he will understand what you mean.

26   One who mistreats his father and evicts his mother
>   is a son who brings them shame and disgrace.

27   My son, if you stop heeding discipline,
>   you will stray from the principles of knowledge.

28   A worthless witness mocks at justice,
>   and the mouth of the wicked swallows wrongdoing.

29   Judgments are in store for scorners
>   and blows for the backs of fools.

20 1   Wine is a mocker, strong liquor a rowdy;
>   anyone led astray by it is unwise.

2   The dread of a king is like when a lion roars;
>   he who makes him angry commits a life-threatening sin.

3   Avoiding quarrels brings a person honor;
>   for any fool can explode in anger.

4   A lazy person won't plow in winter;
>   so at harvest-time, when he looks, there is nothing.

5   The heart's real intentions are like deep water;
>   but a person with discernment draws them out.

6   Most people announce that they show kindness,
>   but who can find someone faithful [enough to do it]?

7   The righteous live a life of integrity;
>   happy are their children after them.

8   The king seated on his judgment throne
>   can winnow out all evil with his glance.

9   Who can say, "I have made my heart clean,
>   I am cleansed from my sin"?

10   False weights and false measures —
>   Adonai detests them both.

11 The character of even a child is known by how he acts,
by whether his deeds are pure and right.

12 The hearing ear and the seeing eye —
ADONAI made them both.

13 If you love sleep, you will become poor;
keep your eyes open, and you'll have plenty of food.

14 "Really bad stuff!" says the buyer [to the seller];
then he goes off and brags [about his bargain].

15 A person may have gold and a wealth of pearls,
but lips informed by knowledge are a precious jewel.

16 Seize his clothes, because he guaranteed a stranger's loan;
take them as security for that unknown woman.

17 Food obtained by fraud may taste good,
but later the mouth is full of gravel.

18 After consultation, plans succeed;
so take wise advice when waging war.

19 A gossip goes around revealing secrets,
so don't get involved with a talkative person.

20 Whoever curses his father or mother —
his lamp will go out in total darkness.

21 Possessions acquired quickly at first
will not be blessed in the end.

22 Don't say, "I'll pay back evil for evil";
wait for ADONAI to save you.

23 ADONAI detests a double standard in weights,
and false scales are not good.

24 A man's steps are ordered by ADONAI,
so how can a person understand his own ways?

25 It is a snare to dedicate a gift to God rashly
and reflect on the vows only afterwards.

26 A wise king winnows the wicked [from the righteous]
and threshes them under the cartwheel.

27 The human spirit is a lamp of *Adonai*;
        it searches one's inmost being.

28 Grace and truth preserve a king;
        with grace he upholds his throne.

29 The pride of the young is their strength;
        the dignity of the old is gray hair.

30 Blows that wound purge away evil,
        yes, beatings [cleanse] one's inmost being.

21 ¹ The king's heart in *Adonai*'s hand is like streams of water —
        he directs it wherever he pleases.

2   All a person's ways are right in his own view,
        but *Adonai* weighs the heart.

3   To do what is right and just
        is more pleasing to *Adonai* than sacrifice.

4   Haughty looks, a proud heart —
        what the wicked plow is sin.

5   The plans of the diligent lead only to abundance;
        but all who rush in arrive only at want.

6   A fortune gained by a lying tongue
        is vapor dispersed [by] seekers of death.

7   The violence of the wicked will sweep them away,
        because they refuse to act justly.

8   A criminal's conduct is crooked,
        but the work of the pure is right.

9   It is better to live on a corner of the roof
        than to share the house with a nagging wife.

10 The wicked is set on evil;
        he doesn't pity even his neighbor.

11 When a scorner is punished, the simple become wiser;
        and when the wise is instructed, he takes hold of knowledge.

12 The Righteous One observes the house of the wicked;
        he overthrows the wicked to their ruin.

13   Whoever stops up his ears at the cry of the poor
        will himself cry, but not be answered.

14   A secret gift allays anger,
        and a bribe under the cloak the strongest fury.

15   Acting justly is a joy for the righteous
        but it terrifies evildoers.

16   The person who strays from the way of common sense
        will come to rest in the company of the dead.

17   Pleasure-lovers will suffer want;
        he who loves wine and oil won't get rich.

18   The wicked serve as a ransom for the righteous,
        and likewise the perfidious for the upright.

19   It is better to live in the desert
        than with a nagging, irritable wife.

20   In the home of the wise are fine treasures and oil,
        but a fool quickly devours it.

21   He who pursues righteousness and kindness
        finds life, prosperity and honor.

22   A wise man can go up into a city of warriors
        and undermine the strength in which it trusts.

23   Whoever guards his mouth and tongue
        keeps himself out of trouble.

24   "Scoffer" is what you call a proud, insolent person
        who acts with overweening conceit.

25   A lazy man's craving will kill him,
        because his hands refuse to work —
26   he covets greedily all day long;
        but a righteous person gives without holding back.

27   The sacrifice of the wicked is an abomination;
        how much more when he brings it with vile motives.

28   A lying witness is doomed,
        but one who heard [what was said] will testify successfully.

²⁹ A wicked man puts on a bold face,
   whereas the upright prepares his ways.

³⁰ No wisdom, discernment or counsel
   succeeds against ADONAI.

³¹ A horse may be prepared for the day of battle,
   but victory comes from ADONAI.

22¹ Rather than wealth, choose a good reputation,
   esteem over silver and gold.

² Rich and poor have this in common —
   ADONAI made them both.

³ The clever see trouble coming and hide;
   the simple go on and pay the penalty.

⁴ The reward for humility is fear of ADONAI,
   along with wealth, honor and life.

⁵ Thorns and snares beset the way of the stubborn;
   he who values his life keeps his distance from them.

⁶ Train a child in the way he [should] go;
   and, even when old, he will not swerve from it.

⁷ The rich rule the poor,
   and the borrower is slave to the lender.

⁸ He who sows injustice reaps trouble,
   and the rod of his angry outburst will fail.

⁹ He who is generous is blessed,
   because he shares his food with the poor.

¹⁰ Throw the scoffer out, and quarreling goes too;
   strife and insults cease.

¹¹ He who loves the pure-hearted and is gracious in speech
   will have the king as his friend.

¹² The eyes of ADONAI protect [the man with] knowledge,
   but he overturns the plans of a traitor.

¹³ A lazy man says, "There's a lion outside!
   I'll be killed if I go out in the street!"

14   The mouth of an adulteress is a deep pit;
        the man with whom ADONAI is angry falls into it.

15   Doing wrong is firmly tied to the heart of a child,
        but the rod of discipline will drive it far away from him.

16   Both oppressing the poor to enrich oneself
        and giving to the rich yield only loss.

17   Pay attention, and listen to the words of the wise;
        apply your heart to my knowledge;
18   for it is pleasant to keep them deep within you;
        have all of them ready on your lips.
19   I want your trust to be in ADONAI;
        this is why I'm instructing you about them today.
20   I have written you worthwhile things
        full of good counsel and knowledge,
21   so you will know that these sayings are certainly true
        and bring back true sayings to him who sent you.

22   Don't exploit the helpless, because they are helpless,
        and don't crush the poor in court,
23   for ADONAI will plead their case for them
        and withhold life from those who defraud them.

24   Don't associate with an angry man;
        make no hot-tempered man your companion.
25   If you do, you may learn his ways
        and find yourself caught in a trap.

26   Don't be one of those who give pledges,
        guaranteeing loans made to others;
27   for if you don't have the wherewithal to pay,
        they will take your bed away from underneath you.

28   Don't move the ancient boundary stone
        set up by your ancestors.

29   Do you see a man skilled at his work?
        He will serve kings, not obscure people.

23 1   When you sit down to dine with a ruler,
        think carefully about who is before you.
2   If you have a big appetite,
        put a knife to your throat!
3   Don't be greedy for his delicacies,
        for they are deceptive food.

190

4   Don't exhaust yourself in pursuit of wealth;
        be smart enough to desist.
5   If you make your eyes rush at it,
        it's no longer there!
    For wealth will surely grow wings,
        like an eagle flying off to the sky.

6   Don't eat the food of a stingy man;
        don't be greedy for his delicacies.
7   For he is like someone who keeps accounts —
    "Eat! Drink!" he says to you,
        but he doesn't really mean it.
8   The little you eat you will vomit up,
        and your compliments will have been wasted.

9   Don't speak in the ears of a fool,
        for he will only despise the common sense in your words.

10   Don't move the ancient boundary stone
        or encroach on the land of the fatherless;
11   for their Redeemer is strong;
        he will take up their fight against you.

12   Apply your mind to discipline
        and your ears to words of knowledge.

13   Don't withhold discipline from a child —
        if you beat him with a stick, he won't die!
14   If you beat him with a stick,
        you will save him from Sh'ol.

15   My son, if your heart is wise,
        then my own heart too is glad;
16   my inmost being rejoices
        when your lips say what is right.

17   Don't envy sinners, but follow the example
        of those who always fear God;
18   for then you will have a future;
        what you hope for will not be cut off.

19   You, my son: listen, be wise,
        and set your mind on the right way.

20   Don't be one of those who guzzle wine
        or of those who eat meat to excess,
21   for both drunkard and glutton will become poor —
        drowsiness will clothe them with rags.

22   Listen to your father, who gave you life;
        and don't despise your mother when she gets old.

23   Buy the truth, don't sell it,
        also wisdom, discipline and discernment.

24   A righteous person's father will be filled with joy;
        yes, he whose son is wise will rejoice in him.
25   So let your father and mother be glad;
        let her who gave you birth rejoice.

26   My son, give me your heart;
        let your eyes observe my ways.

27   A prostitute is a deep ditch,
        and a forbidden woman like a narrow well.
28   She lies in wait to snatch her prey
        and adds to the number of faithless men.

29   Who has misery? Who has regret?
        Who fights and complains all the time?
    Who gets bruised for no good reason?
        Who has bloodshot eyes?
30   Those who spend their time over wine,
        those always trying out mixed drinks.
31   Don't gaze at the red wine
        as it gives its color to the cup.
    It may glide down smoothly now;
32   but in the end, it bites like a serpent —
        yes, it strikes like a poisonous snake.
33   Your eyes will see peculiar things,
        your mind will utter nonsense.
34   You will feel as if lying on the waves of the sea
        or sprawled on top of the mast —
35   "They hit me, but I didn't feel it!
        They beat me up, and I didn't even know it!
    When will I wake up? . . .
        I'll go get another drink."

24 ¹   Don't be envious of evil people,
        and don't desire to be with them.
2   For their minds are occupied with violence,
        and their lips speak of making trouble.

3   By wisdom a house is built,
        by understanding it is made secure,

4   and by knowledge its rooms are filled
         with all kinds of costly and pleasant possessions.

5   A wise man is strong;
         yes, a man of knowledge grows in strength.
6   For with clever strategy you wage your war,
         and victory comes from having many advisers.

7   Wisdom is too lofty for a fool;
         he keeps his mouth shut at the city gate.

8   He who plans to do evil
         people call a schemer.

9   The evil plans of the foolish are sin,
         and people detest a scorner.

10   If you slack off on a day of distress,
         your strength is small indeed.
11   Yes, rescue those being dragged off to death —
         won't you save those about to be killed?
12   If you say, "We knew nothing about it,"
         won't he who weighs hearts discern it?
     Yes, he who guards you will know it
         and repay each one as his deeds deserve.

13   My son, eat honey, for it is good;
         honeycomb drippings are sweet to your taste.
14   Know that wisdom is similar[ly sweet] to your soul;
         if you find it, then you will have a future,
         what you hope for will not be cut off.

15   Don't lurk like an outlaw near the home of the righteous,
         don't raid the place where he lives.
16   For though he falls seven times, he will get up again;
         it's the wicked who fail under stress.

17   Don't rejoice when your enemy falls;
         don't let your heart be glad when he stumbles.
18   For ADONAI might see it, and it would displease him;
         he might withdraw his anger from your foe.

19   Don't get upset because of evildoers;
         don't be envious of the wicked.
20   For the evil person has no future —
         the lamp of the wicked will go out.

²¹   My son, don't get involved with revolutionaries,
        but fear ADONAI and the king.
²²   For disaster from them will suddenly appear,
        and who knows what ruin they both can cause?

²³ These also are sayings of the wise:

    Showing partiality in judgment is not good.
²⁴   He who tells the guilty, "You are innocent,"
        will be cursed by peoples, reviled by nations;
²⁵   but with those who condemn him, things will go well,
        and a good blessing will come upon them.

²⁶   Giving an honest answer
        is like giving a kiss.

²⁷   Prepare your outside work,
    and get things ready for yourself on the land;
        after that, build your house.

²⁸   Don't be a witness against your neighbor for no reason —
        would you use your lips to deceive?

²⁹   Don't say, "I'll do to him what he did to me,
        I'll pay him back what his deeds deserve."

³⁰   I passed by the field of the lazy man
        and the vineyard of the man lacking sense.
³¹   There it was, overgrown with thistles;
        the ground was covered with nettles,
        and its stone wall was broken down.
³²   I looked, and I thought about it;
        I saw, and I learned this lesson:
³³   "I'll just lie here a bit, rest a little longer,
        just fold my hands for a little more sleep" —
³⁴   and poverty comes marching in on you,
        scarcity hits you like an invading soldier.

25 ¹ These also are proverbs of Shlomo; the men of Hizkiyah king of Y'hudah copied them out:

²   God gets glory from concealing things;
        kings get glory from investigating things.
³   Like the sky for height or the earth for depth
        is the heart of kings — unfathomable.
⁴   Remove the impurities from the silver,
        and the smith has material to make a vessel.

5 Remove the wicked from the king's presence,
    and his throne will rest firmly on righteousness.
6 Don't put yourself forward in the king's presence;
    don't take a place among the great.
7 For it is better to be told, "Come up here,"
    than be degraded in the presence of a nobleman.

    What your eyes have seen,
8   don't rush to present in a dispute.
    For what will you do later on,
    if your neighbor puts you to shame?
9 Discuss your dispute with your neighbor,
    but don't reveal another person's secrets.
10 If you do, and he hears of it, he will disgrace you,
    and your bad reputation will stick.

11 Like apples of gold in settings of silver
    is a word appropriately spoken.
12 Like a gold earring, like a fine gold necklace
    is a wise reprover to a receptive ear.
13 Like the coldness of snow in the heat of the harvest
    is a faithful messenger to the one who sends him;
    he refreshes his master's spirit.
14 Like clouds and wind that bring no rain
    is he who boasts of gifts he never gives.

15 With patience a ruler may be won over,
    and a gentle tongue can break bones.

16 If you find honey, eat only what you need;
    for if you eat too much of it, you may throw it up;
17 so don't visit your neighbor too much,
    or he may get his fill of you and come to hate you.

18 Like a club, a sword or a sharp arrow
    is a person who gives false testimony against a neighbor.

19 Relying on an untrustworthy person in a time of trouble
    is like [relying on] a broken tooth or an unsteady leg.

20 Like removing clothes on a chilly day or like vinegar on soda
    is someone who sings songs to a heavy heart.

21 If someone who hates you is hungry, give him food to eat;
    and if he is thirsty, give him water to drink.
22 For you will heap fiery coals [of shame] on his head,
    and *Adonai* will reward you.

23 The north wind brings rain
   and a backbiting tongue, angry looks.

24 It is better to live on a corner of the roof
   than to share the house with a nagging wife.

25 Like cold water to a person faint from thirst
   is good news from a distant land.

26 Like a muddied spring or a polluted well
   is a righteous person who gives way before the wicked.

27 It isn't good to eat too much honey
   or to seek honor after honor.

28 Like a city breached, without walls,
   is a person who lacks self-control.

26 ¹ Like snow in summer or rain at harvest-time,
   so honor for a fool is out of place.

2 Like a fluttering sparrow or a flying swallow,
   an undeserved curse will come home to roost.

3 A whip for a horse, a bridle for a donkey,
   and a rod for the back of fools.

4 Don't answer a fool in terms of his folly,
   or you will be descending to his level;

5 but answer a fool as his folly deserves,
   so that he won't think he is wise.

6 Telling a message to a fool and sending him out
   is like cutting off one's feet and drinking violence.

7 The legs of the disabled hang limp and useless;
   likewise a proverb in the mouth of a fool.

8 Like one who ties his stone to the sling
   is he who gives honor to a fool.

9 Like a thorn branch in the hand of a drunk
   is a proverb in the mouth of a fool.

10 A master can make anything,
   but hiring a fool is like hiring some passer-by.

11 Just as a dog returns to his vomit,
   a fool repeats his folly.

12 Do you see someone who thinks himself wise?
   There is more hope for a fool than for him!

13 The lazy person says, "There's a lion in the streets!
   A lion is roaming loose out there!"

14   The door turns on its hinges,
    and the lazy man on his bed.
15   The lazy person buries his hand in the dish
    but is too tired to return it to his mouth.
16   A lazy man is wiser in his own view
    than seven who can answer with sense.

17   Like someone who grabs a dog by the ears
    is a passer-by who mixes in a fight not his own.

18   Like a madman shooting deadly arrows and firebrands
19   is one who deceives another, then says, "It was just a joke."

20   If there's no wood, the fire goes out;
    if nobody gossips, contention stops.
21   As coals are to embers and wood to fire
    is a quarrelsome person to kindling strife.

22   A slanderer's words are tasty morsels;
    they slide right down into the belly.

23   Like silver slag overlaid on a clay pot
    are lips that burn [with friendship] over a hating heart.
24   He who hates may hide it with his speech;
    but inside, he harbors deceit.
25   He may speak pleasantly, but don't trust him;
    for seven abominations are in his heart.
26   His hatred may be concealed by deceit,
    but his wickedness will be revealed in the assembly.

27   Whoever digs a pit will fall into it,
    and a stone will come back on the one who starts it rolling.
28   A lying tongue hates its victims,
    and a flattering mouth causes ruin.

27 1   Don't boast about tomorrow,
    for you don't know what the day may bring.

2   Let someone else praise you, not your own mouth,
    a stranger and not your own lips.

3   Stone is heavy and sand a dead weight,
    but a fool's provocation outweighs them both.

4   Fury is cruel and anger overwhelming,
    but who can stand up to jealousy?

5   Better open rebuke
        than hidden love.

6   Wounds from a friend are received as well-meant,
        but an enemy's kisses are insincere.

7   A person who is full loathes a honeycomb;
        but to the hungry, any bitter thing is sweet.

8   Like a bird that strays from its nest
        is a man who strays from his home.

9   Perfume and incense make the heart glad,
        [also] friendship sweet with advice from the heart.

10   Don't abandon a friend
        who is also a friend of your father.

     Don't enter your brother's house on the day of your calamity —
        better a neighbor nearby than a brother far away.

11   My son, become wise, and gladden my heart,
        so that I can answer my critics.

12   The clever see trouble coming and hide;
        the thoughtless go on and pay the penalty.

13   Seize his clothes because he guaranteed a stranger's loan;
        take them as security for that unknown woman.

14   Whoever greets his neighbor in a loud voice at dawn
        might just as well have cursed him.

15   A leak that keeps dripping on a rainy day
        and the nagging of a wife are the same —
16   whoever can restrain her can restrain the wind
        or keep perfume on his hand from making itself known.

17   Just as iron sharpens iron,
        a person sharpens the character of his friend.

18   Whoever tends the fig tree will eat its fruit,
        and he who is attentive to his master will be honored.

19   Just as water reflects the face,
        so one human heart reflects another.

20 Sh'ol and Abaddon are never satisfied,
    and human eyes are never satisfied.

21 The crucible [tests] silver, and the furnace [tests] gold,
    but a person [is tested] by [his reaction to] praise.

22 You can crush a fool in a mortar with a pestle,
    along with the grain being crushed;
        yet his foolishness will not leave him.

23 Take care to know the condition of your flocks,
    and pay attention to your herds.
24 For wealth doesn't last forever,
        neither does a crown through all generations.
25 When the hay has been mown, and the new grass appears,
        and the mountain greens have been gathered;
26 the lambs will provide your clothing,
        the goats will sell for enough to buy a field,
27 and there will be enough goat's milk
        to [buy] food for you and your household
        and maintenance for your servant-girls.

28 1 The wicked flee when no one pursues them;
        but the righteous, like lions, feel sure of themselves.

2 A land which transgresses [is punished by] having many rulers;
        but with a man of understanding and knowledge, stability is prolonged.

3 A poor man who oppresses the weak
        is like a downpour that sweeps away all the food.

4 Those who abandon *Torah* praise the wicked,
        but those who keep *Torah* fight them.

5 Evil people don't understand justice,
        but those who seek *Adonai* understand everything.

6 Better to be poor and live an honest life
        than be crooked in one's ways, though rich.

7 A wise son observes *Torah*,
        but a friend of those lacking restraint shames his father.

8 He who increases his wealth by charging exorbitant interest
        amasses it for someone who will bestow it on the poor.

9   If a person will not listen to *Torah*,
         even his prayer is an abomination.

10   Whoever causes the honest to pursue evil ways
     will himself fall into his own pit,
         but the pure-hearted will inherit good.

11   The rich man is wise in his own view,
         but the poor who has discernment sees through him.

12   When the just are triumphant, there is great rejoicing,
         but when the wicked rise up, people hide.

13   He who conceals his sins will not succeed;
         he who confesses and abandons them will gain mercy.

14   Happy the person who is never without fear,
         but he who hardens his heart will fall into misfortune.

15   Like a roaring lion or a bear prowling for food
         is a wicked ruler over a poor people.

16   A prince without discernment is a cruel oppressor,
         but one who hates greed will prolong his life.

17   Let a man weighed down with anyone's blood
         flee to a pit; give him no support.

18   Whoever lives blamelessly will be saved,
         but he whose ways are crooked will fall in one [of those ways].

19   He who farms his land will have plenty of food,
         but he who follows futilities will have plenty of poverty.
20   A trustworthy person will receive many blessings,
         but one rushing to get rich will not go unpunished.

21   To show partiality is not good,
         though a person may do wrong for a crust of bread.

22   He who is greedy rushes after riches,
         not knowing that want will overtake him.

23   He who rebukes another person
         in the end gets more thanks than the flatterer.

24   Whoever robs mother or father and says, "That's not a crime!"
         is comrade to the destroyer.

²⁵ A grasping disposition stirs up strife,
but he who trusts in *Adonai* will prosper.

²⁶ He who trusts in himself is a fool,
but he who lives by wisdom will escape.

²⁷ He who gives to the poor will lack nothing,
but he who hides his eyes will get curses in plenty.

²⁸ When the wicked rise up, people hide;
but when they perish, the righteous flourish.

29 ¹ He who remains stiffnecked after much rebuke
will be suddenly and incurably broken.

² When the righteous flourish, the people rejoice;
but when the wicked are in power, the people groan.

³ Whoever loves wisdom brings joy to his father,
but a patron of prostitutes wastes his wealth.

⁴ A king gives stability to a country by justice,
but one who overtaxes it brings it to ruin.

⁵ A person who flatters his neighbor
spreads a net for his own steps.

⁶ In an evil person's crime is a trap,
but the righteous sing and rejoice.

⁷ The righteous understands the cause of the poor,
but the wicked is unconcerned.

⁸ Scoffers can inflame a city,
but the wise can calm the fury.

⁹ When a wise man argues with a foolish one,
he meets anger and ridicule without relief.

¹⁰ Men of blood hate those who are pure
and seek the life of the upright.

¹¹ A fool gives vent to all his feelings,
but the wise, thinking of afterwards, stills them.

¹² If a ruler listens to lies,
all his officials will be wicked.

13   The poor and the oppressor have this in common:
      Adonai gives light to the eyes of both.

14   If a king steadfastly gives justice to the poor,
      his throne will be secure forever.

15   The rod and rebuke give wisdom,
      but a child left to himself brings shame on his mother.

16   When the wicked flourish, wrongdoing flourishes;
      but the righteous will witness their downfall.

17   Discipline your son, and he will give you rest;
      yes, he will be your delight.

18   Without a prophetic vision, the people throw off all restraint;
      but he who keeps *Torah* is happy.

19   A slave can't be disciplined with words;
      he may understand, but he won't respond.

20   Do you see someone too anxious to speak?
      There is more hope for a fool than for him.

21   A slave who is pampered from youth
      will in the end be ungrateful.

22   Angry people stir up strife;
      hot-tempered people commit many crimes.

23   The proud will be humbled,
      but the humble will be honored.

24   The accomplice of a thief hates himself;
      he hears himself put under oath but discloses nothing.

25   Fearing human beings is a snare;
      but he who trusts in *Adonai* will be raised high [above danger].

26   Many seek the ruler's favor,
      but it is from *Adonai* that each gets justice.

27   An unjust person is an abomination to the righteous,
      but he who lives uprightly is an abomination to the wicked.

30 ^{1} The words of Agur the son of Yakeh, the prophecy. The man says to Iti'el, to Iti'el and Ukhal:

^{2} I am more boorish than anyone,
                I lack human discernment;
^{3} I have not learned enough wisdom
                to know the Holy One.

^{4} Who has gone up to heaven and come down?
            Who has cupped the wind in the palms of his hands?
            Who has wrapped up the waters in his cloak?
            Who established all the ends of the earth?
            What is his name, and what is his son's name?
            Surely you know!

^{5} Every word of God's is pure;
                he shields those taking refuge in him.
^{6} Don't add anything to his words;
                or he will rebuke you, and you be found a liar.

^{7} [God,] I have asked two things of you;
                don't deny them to me as long as I live —
^{8} keep falsehood and futility far from me,
                and give me neither poverty nor wealth.
            Yes, provide just the food I need today;
^{9} for if I have too much, I might deny you
                and say, "Who is ADONAI?"
            And if I am poor, I might steal
                and thus profane the name of my God.

^{10} Never disparage a slave to his master,
                or he will curse you, and you will deserve it.

^{11} There is a type of people who curse their fathers
                and don't bless their mothers.
^{12} There is a type of people clean in their own view,
                but not cleansed from their filth.
^{13} There is a type of people — how haughty their look! —
                utterly supercilious!
^{14} There is a type of people whose teeth are like swords,
                yes, their fangs are knives;
            they devour the poor from the earth,
                the needy from humankind.

^{15} The leech has two daughters;
                they cry, "Give! Give!"

Three things are never satisfied;
four never say, "Enough!" —
¹⁶
     Sh'ol and a barren womb;
    the earth, never satisfied with water;
    and fire, which never says, "Enough!"

¹⁷
The eye that mocks his father
    and scorns obeying his mother
will be pecked out by the ravens in the valley,
    and the vultures will eat it.

¹⁸
Three things are too wonderful for me,
four beyond my knowledge —
¹⁹
    the way of an eagle in the sky,
    the way of a snake on a rock,
    the way of a ship on the open sea,
    and the way of a man with a girl.

²⁰
This is how an unfaithful wife behaves:
    she eats, wipes her mouth, and says, "I did nothing wrong."

²¹
Three things make the earth quake,
four things it can't bear —
²²
    a slave who becomes king,
    a boor gorged with food,
²³
    a hated [wife] when her husband takes her [back],
    and a slave-girl who inherits from her mistress.

²⁴
Four things on the earth are small;
    nevertheless, they are very wise —
²⁵
the ants, a species not strong,
    yet they store up their food in the summer;
²⁶
the coneys, a species with little power,
    yet they make their home in the rocks;
²⁷
the locusts, who have no king,
    yet they all march out in ranks;
²⁸
and the spiders, which you can catch in your hand,
    yet they are in the king's palace.

²⁹
Three things are stately in their stride,
four of stately gait —
³⁰
    the lion, mightiest of beasts,
    which turns aside for no one;
³¹
    the greyhound, the billy-goat
    and the king when his army is with him.

³²   If you have been boorish, exalting yourself,
        or if you have been scheming,
           lay your hand on your mouth.
³³   For as pressing milk produces butter
        and pressing the nose produces blood,
           so pressing out anger produces strife.

31 ¹ The words of King L'mu'el, the prophecy with which his mother disciplined him:

²   No, my son! No, son of my womb!
           No, son of my vows!
³   Don't give your strength to women
           or your ways to that which destroys kings.
⁴   It is not for kings, L'mu'el,
           not for kings to drink wine;
        it is not for rulers to ask,
           "Where can I find strong liquor?"
⁵   For they may drink, then forget what has been decreed,
           and pervert the justice due to the poor.
⁶   Give strong liquor to one who is perishing,
           wine to the deeply depressed;
⁷   let him drink, forget his poverty
           and cease to remember his troubles.

⁸   Speak up for those who can't speak for themselves,
           for the rights of all who need an advocate.
⁹   Speak up, judge righteously,
           defend the cause of the poor and the needy.

א   ¹⁰ Who can find a capable wife?
           Her value is far beyond that of pearls.
ב   ¹¹ Her husband trusts her from his heart,
           and she will prove a great asset to him.
ג   ¹² She works to bring him good, not harm,
           all the days of her life.

ד   ¹³ She procures a supply of wool and flax
           and works with willing hands.
ה   ¹⁴ She is like those merchant vessels,
           bringing her food from far away.
ו   ¹⁵ It's still dark when she rises to give food to her household
           and orders to the young women serving her.

ז   ¹⁶ She considers a field, then buys it,
           and from her earnings she plants a vineyard.

ח   ¹⁷ She gathers her strength around her
          and throws herself into her work.
ט   ¹⁸ She sees that her business affairs go well;
          her lamp stays lit at night.

י   ¹⁹ She puts her hands to the staff with the flax;
          her fingers hold the spinning rod.
כ   ²⁰ She reaches out to embrace the poor
          and opens her arms to the needy.

ל   ²¹ When it snows, she has no fear for her household;
          since all of them are doubly clothed.
מ   ²² She makes her own quilts;
          she is clothed in fine linen and purple.

נ   ²³ Her husband is known at the city gates
          when he sits with the leaders of the land.
ס   ²⁴ She makes linen garments and sells them;
          she supplies the merchants with sashes.

ע   ²⁵ Clothed with strength and dignity,
          she can laugh at the days to come.
פ   ²⁶ When she opens her mouth, she speaks wisely;
          on her tongue is loving instruction.
צ   ²⁷ She watches how things go in her house,
          not eating the bread of idleness.

ק   ²⁸ Her children arise; they make her happy;
          her husband too, as he praises her:
ר   ²⁹ "Many women have done wonderful things,
          but you surpass them all!"

ש   ³⁰ Charm can lie, beauty can vanish,
          but a woman who fears A<small>DONAI</small> should be praised.
ת   ³¹ Give her a share in what she produces;
          let her works speak her praises at the city gates.

Printed in the United States
by Baker & Taylor Publisher Services